My Journey to Blue Sky

Barry Greenfield

NEW HAVEN PUBLISHING

Published 2025
First Edition
New Haven Publishing Ltd
www.newhavenpublishingltd.com newhavenpublishing@gmail.com

All Rights Reserved
The rights of Barry Greenfield as the author of this work, have been asserted in accordance with the Copyrights, Designs and Patents Act 1988.
No part of this book may be re-printed or reproduced or utilized in any form or by any electronic, mechanical or other means, now unknown or hereafter invented, including photocopying, and recording, or in any information storage or retrieval system, without the written permission of the
Authors and Publisher.

Cover Design © Pete Cunliffe

Copyright © 2025 Barry Greenfield
All rights reserved
ISBN: 978-1-915975-12-6

Dedication

I dedicate this book to Navy, my three year old granddaughter. We play, talk, read, laugh, run, smile, cry, and as we do, I catch glimpses of light emanating from her. Sometimes in her eyes, in her laughter, her hop, her giggle, her way. I see flashes of light. Spiritual light is a metaphorical term, it represents a divine presence, understanding, or guidance, often signifying a connection to a higher power, truth, or wisdom. I have learnt so much from being with her. Her magic, her old-soul knowledge that I have channeled for this book. I love you Navy, Zaida.

I dedicate this book to my beloved wife Lori, without whom I would not have known grace, patience, or hard work. She is my partner in life, and all we do, we do as one. Lori is my inspiration. I love you Lori. Husband.

I dedicate this book to Macartney. My daughter whom I respect, admire, and love without boundary, or the barrier of time. We have stood together for all our lives. A shared journey. I love you Macartney. Dad.

I dedicate this book to the many musicians and songwriters that I have shared space and time with over the years. I am always in school.

Content

Barry Greenfield Acclaim My Journey to Blue Sky   7

Chapters

1 My Journey to Blue Sky Began in Manchester   11
2 Apple Records, John Lennon in London, 1968   22
3 A Friday afternoon with Kenny Rogers in 1969   34
4 The day Cher kissed me (on the cheek) 1970   41
5 10cc, 'Sweet America' my first recording, Stockport 1971   49
6 My first tour   64
7 The recording of Blue Sky in RCA Hollywood 1973   74
8 The afternoon that I met Harry Nilsson and Richard Starkey 1973   90

Photo Gallery

9 Thanksgiving dinner at Mike Nesmith's Home 1973   96
10 The songwriter's triangle, Joni, Buffy and me 1974   104
11 An evening with Supertramp at the Queen Elizabeth Theatre   112
12 The Art of Song Writing – My passion   122
13 The 12 Bar Club, London. 19 September 2006   139
14 'My day in Auschwitz'. Five songs. 2019   148

Tidbits

1 Understanding the greatness that is Nashville 2007
   and 2008   158

2 Some collaborations are platinum.
   Some collaborations are tin   166

3 My weird, short Dylan tale, Sound Emporium Studios,
   Nashville   September 20, 2007   172

4 Graham Nash and Shane Fontayne Tarrytown
   NY 2016   176

5 Taylor Hawkins and David Grohl Heathrow Airport
   Lounge October 2018   181

6 Taylor Hawkins and David Grohl Heathrow Airport
   Lounge October 2018   186

Epilogue   190

Acknowledgements   192

Barry Greenfield Acclaim My Journey to Blue Sky

Record Collector, UK's longest-running music monthly, featured *'Blue Sky'* in a three-page article in its June 2024 issue.

Charles Donovan, Contributing Editor, Record Collector, London, January 2025

When our Canadian correspondent told the Record Collector office about Barry Greenfield – that he was an accomplished singer/songwriter whose career stretched back to teenage interactions with Apple Records, the BBC and Graham Gouldman, and whose 1973 RCA album, Blue Sky, had been unjustly mishandled at the time of its release - it sounded like the perfect story for us. And then, of course, I realised why I already knew him; his songs were on a Buffy Sainte-Marie album I'd had since the 90s. When we listened to Blue Sky we were struck by Barry's thoughtful, poignant, beautifully produced songs, touching on subjects ranging from marital abuse (Free The Lady) to pacifism (Sweet America) and pollution (New York's Closed Tonight) blurring elements of folk, pop, rock, country and jazz. The music was so genial, well-written, intelligent and moving, as if someone had combined the best aspects of John Prine and Cat Stevens; no wonder Apple had wanted him on the basis of a quick, unscheduled audition.

Since the article came out, I've got to know more about Barry; he seems to be someone untouched by cynicism, earnest in the very best possible sense of the word, whose life in music has been motivated by nothing other than the desire to share his gifts; no overbearing ego, no yearning for fame as a substitute for self-esteem. No wonder people speak so highly not just of his talent, but of his character. He's also a mine of music business stories and anecdotes. The two of us who got to meet him through RC – writer Joe Isaacs and me - are both the richer for it. We're so glad that more and more people are finding out about his work.

Joe Isaacs, UK Music Journalist, *Record Collector, London, June 2024*

'Barry Greenfield might just be the best songwriter you've probably never heard of. The English-born Canadian had a BBC Record of the Week back in 1970 with the Vietnam War protest song "Sweet America", which also went to number one in England, followed by another number one in 1972 with "New York is Closed Tonight". This productive run of form culminated in 1973 with Greenfield's first studio album, Blue Sky, a little-known piece of 1970s folk–pop-rock that has stood the test of time lyrically and musically, a record which captures an artist on the precipice of major commercial and critical success. Except that success never came. The album was never released. A true maverick, Greenfield recorded a seminal album of the singer-songwriter genre and vanished into the ether, with all twenty copies of Blue Sky that were ever printed and left the business. 50 years later, Blue Sky is being re-released by Greenfield in light of the steadily growing attention it has received in the ensuing decades.'

David M. Kershenbaum, Producer, Record Executive.

'You are very talented Barry, wonderful songs, fabulous voice and we both benefited from the best studio musicians and recording studios in the industry at that time. It's not a surprise that Blue Sky still endures.'

Graham Gouldman, Musician, singer and songwriter, 10cc wrote:

'I was 24, and Barry was 19, when we met in 1970. He was introduced to me by my then manager Harvey Lisberg (Herman's Hermits). Lisberg thought Barry's songwriting, and voice, were unusually strong and interesting, and suggested to me that he may be a good addition to Kennedy Street Enterprises. Lisberg wanted my opinion. I drove over to listen to this young Canadian. Barry sang me some songs. I liked his original style and strong lyrics. I agreed to work with him on the spot.

It's wonderful that Barry is writing a book, 'My Journey to Blue Sky'. Barry has a great history, that includes working, and meeting, with many great musicians on the way.'

Robert Williston, The Museum of Canadian Music:
The Museum of Canadian Music added BLUE SKY to the collection of Canadian Recordings. THE MUSEUM, the largest Music internet presence in Canada (opened in 1988) wrote, **'Barry Greenfield's 1973 'Blue Sky', is one of the best Canadian albums ever recorded.** Barry Greenfield made an important contribution to Canadian music.

Clay St. Thomas - BCAB Broadcast Performer of the Year/Actor/Voice Artist
Barry Greenfield is a musical mystery a la "Searching for Sugar Man". Like Rodriguez (of the 2013 hit movie), he's maybe the best should've-been-famous singer/songwriter you've never heard of...yet. As Barry's book "My Journey to Blue Sky" reveals, music titans from John Lennon to John Lee Hooker have recognized there's something very special about his music. And like all great songwriters, man, does he know how to tell a story. These are incredible remembrances of A-listers met in a life that criss-crossed generations of popular music.

Dr. Bruce Lipton, PhD, cell biologist and lecturer, an internationally recognized leader in bridging science and spirit, wrote in his May 2024 Newsletter:
'Years of lecturing around this beautiful planet have provided me an opportunity to encounter wonderful Cultural Creatives that are helping to bring harmony into the world. I'd like to introduce you to a wonderful singer-songwriter and someone who I'm blessed to know, Barry Greenfield, who is celebrating the 50th anniversary of his RCA LP BLUE SKY'.

Chris Nole, pianist, songwriter, performer, and music producer wrote:
'I met Barry at a downtown dinner here in Nashville where he happened to be with a mutual friend of ours. I remember my first impression of him was

how upbeat, and enthusiastic he was about the music business. Barry seemed to have a twinkle in his eye when he talked about writing songs. I would later learn of his accomplished and fascinating music career. Not long after our meeting at the diner, Barry contacted me about recording some of his tunes. I called on a few of my favorite session players and booked one of the finest studios here in Nashville for this eclectic artist. Over the years we've cut many superb tracks together - and co-wrote a few groovy songs. In my book, Barry Greenfield's story is what makes him a legend in the music biz, and his love for singing a poignant lyric with his gritty vocals is what makes him stand out still today. May your twinkle continue to shine my friend.

1

My Journey to Blue Sky Began in Manchester
The Kinks, The Who, The Beatles, The Hollies and Bob Dylan.
December 20th, 1963

Music is the shadow in my daily walk, music is the stool on which I sit, music is the pillow for my nightly sleep. Music is where I have gone all my life to find solace, to seek clarity. Music is how I express my heart, my art, and with songwriting I can show my inner thoughts with others.

St. Thomas Aquinas, a renowned Italian philosopher, from the Kingdom of Sicily, 1225-1274, explained that there is a first cause, or prime mover, that is the origin of everything. I discovered my first cause in music in 1963 while listening to a transistor radio in our Salisbury kitchen. That is where I heard The Beatles chart-topper, *'Please Please Me'*. I sat frozen, altered forever.

> *Come on (come on)*
> *Come on (come on)*
> *Come on (come on)*
> *Come on (come on)*
> *Please, please me, whoa, yeah, like I please you*

I was born in 1950, Manchester, England, and I lived my first 7 years as a Mancunian. I loved my Family; I was graced with good mates. I was safe. I loved my home at twenty-one Kendall Road. I was happy at Bowker Vale Primary, and though we had little, we always had enough.

Then on a rainy morning on November 27th, 1958, at age 7, without notice, I was seat-belted on a BOAC Vickers Viscount, a four-engine turboprop airliner, at Manchester Ringway Airport, on a plane bound for Africa. It was a twenty-three-hour flight, with thirteen stops, including London, Lisbon, and Nairobi. The shock of this event felt somewhat like the swift removal of a band-aid. It was a grueling flight. On arrival I decided to date-stamp the moment, I glanced at my Timex on my left wrist, and spoke aloud to no one but me,

'It's 7.28pm, 28 November 1958, and I'm in Salisbury'.

My mother was distraught, an emotion that lingered for life, at being taken from the warm breasts of her sisters. It was a unilateral decision by my father. I never settled in Africa.

Ninety-five percent of the population in Rhodesia, were Africans. The Shona made up three-quarters of the African population, and the Ndebele made up most of the remaining. They provided cheap labour for the five percent, the white Rhodesian Elite. It was wrong.

In 1963, I reached my *tipping point,* and I knew I had to change the picture. It was my *'annus horribilis'.* I was a small, shy, and scared boy. That entire year I was petrified to go to school. I was caned by teachers and beaten by antisemitic older kids. I have always been, and remain, a person who acts on a dilemma, I never succumb.

I had an answer.

'I want to go to Manchester and live with Aunt Sadie and do my schooling in England'.

I left for Aunt Sadie's, via Orly and Heathrow. I was a thirteen-year-old who travelled unaccompanied five thousand miles north, without world, street, or travel experience. I had begun my journey to *'Blue Sky'.* I left family for the unknown. Courage and chance often are ignored, but if followed can result in big change.

Back in Manchester, my mojo came alive. The key to my inner-peace and bliss, was found in music, which was developing into a profound art form in the early sixties. The Kinks, The Who, The Beatles, The Hollies and Bob Dylan. I loved this exciting period. So much talent on display, blossoming everywhere. The songs filled my head. The attitude burnt inside my soul. I understood these musicians. They understood me. They were the roots of the tree. In my heart I felt a shift, I had begun my journey to music. I had begun my journey to *Blue Sky.*

A large amount of that music was important to my development. In fact it was motivating. I would listen intensely, it was never background, it was in-my-face. But five acts stood atop Everest, The Kinks, The Who, The Beatles, The Hollies and Bob Dylan.

The Kinks. Ray Davies. They touched me with their constant reflection of English culture and lifestyle. Ray had a satirical bent, an innate intelligence, and a unique idea which he beautifully translated via his songs. In 1964 they topped all the charts with '*You Really Got Me*'.

Girl, you really got me going
You got me so I don't know what I'm doing
Yeah, you really got me now
You got me so I can't sleep at night

Yeah, you really got me now
You got me so I don't know what I'm doing, now
Oh, yeah, you really got me now
You got me so I can't sleep at night
You really got me

The loud, distorted guitar was soulfully played by Ray's brother, Dave. He achieved this sound by cutting a slice in the speaker cone of his Elpico amplifier, aka *'the little green amp'*. It sounded so fresh on my little transistor. I would wait and wait for the radio to revisit this classic. I would push the volume to maximum and hold it against my ear. I never bought singles in this period. My only companion was the radio.

The Kinks never let up. *'All Day and all of the Night'*, *'Tired of Waiting'*, *'Till the End of the Day'* all were perfect radio singles. Later they would mature and go even deeper with *'Waterloo Sunset'*, *'Victoria'* and the masterpiece *'Lola'*. What an innovative lyric was *'Lola'*. The song details a romantic encounter in a bar in deep dark Soho, between a young man and Lola, who is possibly a transvestite, or a cross dresser. In the poetic lyric Ray describes confusion about Lola,

*She walked up to me and she asked me to dance.
I asked her her name and in a dark brown voice
She said Lola'.
Well, I'm not the world's most physical guy
But when she squeezed me tight she nearly broke my spine
Oh my Lola
La-la-la-la Lola
Well, I'm not dumb but I can't understand
Why she walk like a woman and talk like a man
Oh my Lola
La-la-la-la Lola*

The Kinks members, like Creedence and Pink Floyd, matched the artistry of the leader. Making the whole bigger than the parts.

The Kinks taught me that any topic, any subject, was fair game. A three-minute song can be about day to day events, insights into human behaviour. It need not only be about a lover or dancing. It can be a glimpse of the world. A deep glance into the neighbourhood, in his case Muswell Hill.

The Who. Pete Townsend. They touched me with their power, their volume, and their bravery. I listened to The Who on Radio Caroline. The BBC did not feature much pop music at that time, but the Pirate Radio stations did. Like so many other British teens, I would lie in bed with my transistor radio, faking sleep, listening to The Who *'Anyway, Anyhow, Anywhere'*. It was early 1965, and I kept thinking 'what a great title'. But they surpassed it with the next single, *'My Generation'*, a powerhouse of a record with a first for me, a bass solo from John Entwistle. It used a stutter vocal and two, yes two, key changes. The highlight for me was Pete's line, *'Hope I die before I get old'*. Hit after hit followed, *'I'm a Boy'*, *'Pictures of Lily'*. They are still relevant today. But the tour de force was *'I Can See for Miles'*. To me it is the perfect Who selection. It has it all. Power in its centre, great vocals and backing vocals, and perfect band cohesion. Long but not long enough. Paul McCartney created *'Helter Skelter'* to give The Beatles *that heavy sound*. They both are marvellous. Equals.

The Eiffel Tower and the Taj Mahal
are mine to see on clear days
You thought that I would need a crystal ball
to see right through the haze
Well, here's a poke at you
You're gonna choke on it too
You're gonna lose that smile
Because all the while
I can see for miles and miles

The Who taught me that you can have three geniuses in a Band and a lead vocalist, and it will work. Townsend is my favourite guitarist, Entwistle my #1 bass player, and Moon is Moon. Daltrey never felt right to me, but that's my own personal view which many I am sure disagree. I love it when Pete sings the occasional lead vocal.

The Beatles. Harrison, Starr, McCartney and Lennon. They touched me with their work ethic. Their courage to try anything new, things untried. They saw no walls, only bridges. Their ability to work as a team, and ignore personality quirks and defects, to make their music stronger. When they were creating, they created. Each owned a veto.

As shared earlier in this chapter, I first heard *'Please Please Me'* while living in Rhodesia in the summer of 1963. It changed my life. My desire to explore and understand The Beatles was a catalyst in my move to Manchester in December of that year.

To this day, I still play The Who, The Kinks, The Stones, The Beach Boys, The Small Faces, The Yardbirds and Dylan. But the difference with The Beatles is that I still study them. Their solo work is a part of my library too. They are simply the cream.

Harrison has always been my main entry point. I believe his first composition, *'Don't Bother Me'*, is the equal of his Mates' tunes. I see him as the ultimate creator. Spirit plays a role. His heart is huge and his talent enormous. I never tire of digging into his work. *'Within You Without You'* from Pepper never grows dated or old. It is a Rembrandt.

Try to realize it's all within yourself
No one else can make you change
And to see you're really only very small
And life flows on within you and without you
We were talking about the love that's gone so cold
And the people who gain the world and lose their soul
They don't know, they can't see, are you one of them?
When you've seen beyond yourself then you may find
Peace of mind is waiting there
And the time will come when you see we're all one
And life flows on within you and without you

Many would consider McCartney the best songwriter of his generation. So many beautiful, well-crafted songs, His classical work, instrumentals home demos and studio LPs are magnificent. Sure, some tracks are not prime, but every submission has solid work. I love them all. My favourite will always be *'Ram'*. The LP where his love for Linda is reflected by her love for Paul.

Speed along the highway, honey I want it my way
But listen to her daddy's song, don't stay out to long
Were just busy hidin', sitting the back seat of my car

Lennon was one of the most gifted musicians of any generation. His uniqueness is unequalled. His uniqueness was unequalled. John was innovative, creative, and new. Not only with his lyrics, but in his hesitations in phrase and chord selection, and subject matter. His finest hour is found on Plastic Ono Band. *'Mother'*, *'Isolation'*, *'God'* and others are brilliant. He is the master of words in music. *'Day in The Life'*, *'Strawberry Fields Forever'*, *'Julia'*, *'Happiness is a Warm Gun'* and *'Help'* are five to begin with.

When I was younger, so much younger than today
I never needed anybody's help in any way
But now these days are gone
I'm not so self assured
And now I find I've changed my mind
And opened up the doors

Help me if you can, I'm feeling down
And I do appreciate you being 'round
Help me get my feet back on the ground
Won't you please, please help me, help me, help me.

Starr is a great drummer. His niceness is a lovely thing to behold. He was important in the pie. His interpretation and percussive additions to *'Ticket to Ride'* and *'Rain'* are simply outstanding. His punkish power and attitude on *'She Loves You'*, the 'Shout Live' medley, from Ready Steady Go, and *'Helter Skelter'* are extraordinary. He's got soul.

As good as all their individual solo music is, and it's very good, the thirteen
LPs in the Beatles canon, are the heart of the matter. The four lads created Socrates, da Vinci and Einstein level art.

The LP most noteworthy, in my humble view, is *'Revolver'*. *'Revolver'* is their seventh studio opus. The album was the Beatles' final recording project before their retirement as live performers and marked the group's most overt use of studio technology to date. They built on the advances of their late 1965 release, another gem, *'Rubber Soul'*. Revolver has diverse musical styles, great new sounds, and very interesting lyrics that broke all the norms that preceded this LP. I have played it constantly over the years, I never tire *of 'Good Day Sunshine'*, *'Got to Get You Into My Life'*, *'Love you To'*, *'And you Bird Can Sing*, *'Here, There, and Everywhere'*, and all the others. Timeless beauty.

To lead a better life
I need my love to be here
Here, making each day of the year
Changing my life with the wave of her hand
Nobody can deny that there's something there
There, running my hands through her hair
Both of us thinking how good it can be
Someone is speaking,
But she doesn't know he's there
I want her everywhere
And if she's beside me, I know I need never care

The Beatles taught me that you must love what you do, to do it. You must like what you do, to do it well. You must think before you share it, to be sure it's ready to share. And most importantly don't worry if they do not like what you did, as long as you did what you like.

The Hollies. Allan Clarke, Tony Hicks and Graham Nash touched me with their British style Everly Brothers harmonies. The Hollies had a non-stop flow of hits during the mid-1960's. Their music was joyful, uplifting, well sung, and expertly played. The band was produced by Ron Richard who had impeccable taste. He recorded them in the same EMI Studios as The Beatles. I fondly recall how happy their records made me feel. The Hollies were the perfect anecdote to the hell I left behind in Rhodesia. The Manchester based band hits included, *'Just One Look'*, a song co-written by Americans Doris Troy and Gregory Carroll in 1963.My favourite, and the key song, to my lifetime relationship with The Hollies, is their perfect version of *'I'm Alive'*, their first of two UK number ones. Clint Ballard penned the tune. The lyrics nailed the exuberance a young male teen would feel when he believed he had met that girl! The songs melody, tight harmonies, and well thought out lyrics, spoke perfectly and clearly to my fourteen year old brain.

Now I can breathe
I can see
I can touch
I can feel
I can taste all the sugar sweetness in your kiss
You give me all the things I've ever missed
I've never felt like this
I'm alive, I'm alive, I'm alive

The Hollies taught me the undeniable importance that one member can play in the overall direction of a band. How without that component, they would lose the magic, weaken the soup. I always knew that Graham Nash was the best thing about The Hollies. When he flew the UK nest for California, and CSN in 1968, it was never the same.

Another classic example of this effect, was when Brian Jones was fired from The Rolling Stones in June 1969. Jones was told by Mick Jagger, Keith Richards, and Charlie Watts that the band would continue without him. They missed him. No one can deny the beauty of *'Sticky Fingers'* and *'Let it Bleed'*, but those LPs were with Mick Taylor, who is a stronger player than both Ron Wood and Kieth Richards. The Jones Lps *'Aftermath'* and *'12 x 5'* are more my cup of tea.

Bob Dylan. Robert Zimmerman touched me with intuitive insight.

His early work, *'Blowing in The Wind'*, *'Masters of War'*, *'Mr. Tambourine Man'*, *'Don't Think Twice It's Aright'*, are Van Gogh. His mastery in saying it clearly, and yet still leaving it open to your personal interpretation, always blew my mind. His voice is simply beautiful. His accompaniment is perfect. His words are interesting. His records are listenable. I love his work.

Bob's best moment is hard to call, but I believe it's *'Blood on the Tracks'*. It was recorded in 1975 and is Bob's fifteenth album. The album's songs have been linked to tensions in Dylan's personal life, including his estrangement from his then-wife Sara. Bob will not comment but says that the tunes are not autobiographical. They do speak clearly to the demise and death of a long relationship. *'Tangled Up In Blue'* and *'If You See Her Say Hello'*, do fit well into that explanation. Sara and Bob have five children. It is a painful, but a real, and honest listen. The decline and fall of a marriage. So many taste it. Bob explained it.

> *If you see her, say hello*
> *She might be in Tangier*
> *She left here last early spring*
> *Is livin' there, I hear*
> *Say for me that I'm all right*
> *Though things get kind of slow*
> *She might think that I've forgotten her*
> *Don't tell her it isn't so*
> *We had a falling-out*
> *Like lovers often will*
> *And to think of how she left that night*
> *It still brings me a chill*

And though our separation
It pierced me to the heart
She still lives inside of me
We've never been apart
If you get close to her
Kiss her once for me
Always have respected her
For doin' what she did and gettin' free

Bob Dylan taught me a great deal about the music business. He is *a song and dance man,* and taught me that making art for art's sake, is what it's all about. Money? Who needs it? The troubadour in him is the troubadour in me.

In 1964 and 1966 British TV was important to me and affected and molded my musical decisions and choices, on my journey to Blue Sky. BBC and ITV showcased all the music. Sometimes live, occasionally lip-synced or mimed. *'Ready, Steady, Go', 'Top of The Pops', 'Juke Box Jury', '5 4 3 2 1', 'Sunday Night at the London Palladium'.* Usually thirty minutes, chocker-block full of great bands, singing their hits. It was something I waited avidly for, as I watched the time slowly creep towards the appointed hour. Waiting to see the way they looked, the way they performed. Sandie Shaw, Cilla Black, The Foremost, Peter and Gordon, The Hollies, The Pretty Things. I was never disappointed. It became my classroom. They became my mentors.

The Kinks, The Who, The Hollies were all great. The Rolling Stones worked well, although I never really connected with Mick. All were superb, but one band was the most special, The Beatles. The Beatles did it better than the others. Lennon was always the one who grabbed my eye. He played his guitar with control and no dance. He played music. The other three were great foils for the magic that John offered to his audience in 1964 and 1965. He was the man.

It was identical on the radio. It all worked. I loved the singles by Manfred Mann, *'Do Wah Diddy Diddy',* The Hollies, 'Look Through Any Window', Peter and Gordon, 'W*orld Without Love',* but when I heard *'She Loves You'* and *'From Me to You'* all the others were a bit less. Marginal, yes, but noticeable.

I am a songwriter today because of these formative years. I studied and learnt from The Kinks, The Who, The Beatles, The Hollies and Bob Dylan.

We all have mentors, motivators and those that inspire us. We all seek to emulate, to learn to grow. It's the people that we choose that result in where we go, what we became. A half a degree difference in the rudder, and the boat goes to a different destination.

As Paul McCartney once said,

'If you're going to steal, steal from the best!

Looking back at the root of it all, 1964, 1965, 1966, it was The Kinks, The Who, The Beatles, The Hollies and Bob Dylan that made this boy the man he is today. A musician, a songwriter, a dad, a husband, a friend and a grandpa. They showed me the yellow brick road that took me on my journey to *Blue Sky*.

Footnote:

The music that shapes our souls, if we allow that, can be present in many colours. Pop, R and B, Gospel, Soul, EDM, Classical, Punk, Country. It matters not. What reaches your inner soul is what reaches your inner soul.

2

Apple Records, John Lennon in London, 1968

I was 17. My Grade 12 schedule was always hectic in Grade 12 in Vancouver. The curriculum in 1968 was Math, Biology, English Literature, History, PE, and Physics. I liked my years in school. I enjoyed learning. Friendships. It was an average Tuesday for me.

It was 14 May, and I was on the Student Council committee. I was the student who booked local bands to play in the School Auditorium each month, on the first Tuesday. Music for the kids as they munched on lunch. An escape into dreamland from the ordinary.

1968 was a year filled with good music, played by rag tag, but serious musicians that had learnt their crafts by studying the radio bands of the day. Jefferson Airplane, The Kinks, and The Yardbirds. The school buzzed all morning, awaiting the '*Rock at Lunch Show*'. I could choose from a bunch of strong local units, all eager to perform in our auditorium that sat two hundred. Including Papa Bear's Medicine Show, Spring and Tomorrow's Eyes. A musical way to escape the school day.

The concert was a success, a standing ovation, and the noon-hour soon morphed into late afternoon. As the sun sets, here comes the night. Tonight was going to be exceptional. At midnight John Lennon and Paul McCartney were the guests on '*The Tonight Show on NBC*'. My gurus. My mentors. My true inspiration. Yabba dabba doo.

George, my favorite Beatle, was not expected, but that's OK, I was not greedy. I was nervous all that day, in anticipation of the upcoming event. To hear and see the duo in this unusual, unprecedented environment was a thrilling prospect. They had never been guests on a US TV Talk Show before. Plus, they were without George and Ringo, so they were not performing Beatles songs, just talking, an unusual moment in their journey. A rare treat.

On 9 February 1964, The Beatles performed on the Ed Sullivan Show, but I was living in Zimbabwe at that time, now I was living in Canada. In Canada I got more of my beloved music. Music was the most important aspect in my life, as a 17-year-old.

Midnight came. Mom, Dad, Suzan, all in our pajamas, sat huddled around the box. Cocoa in hand.

'*Barry you're too close to the screen*', my mother would always say.

'*No Mom, I need to be as close to Paul and John as possible*'.

The host that night was Joe Garagiola, not Johnny Carson. A surprise to me, and as I read decades later, a surprise too for the greatest songwriting team of their day. They were expecting Johnny. What a weird call by the NBC Tonight Show staff. The '*B team*' for the elite of guests. A few minutes after midnight the dynamic duo walked through the iconic stage curtain, and into our living rooms.

Looking a bit out of place, Garagiola, an ex-baseball catcher, and Tallulah Bankhead, a forgotten actress, waited on the set. The Tonight Show Band struck up a schmaltzy version of a Beatles classic, perhaps '*I Want To Your Hand*', the Lads walked through the curtain. Waving, smiling, outrageous to witness. I recall watching Elvis light up the screen in GI Blues and feeling the same sense of awe. Overwhelming joy ran through my body. I got goose bumps.

The Boys looked older than the Mop Tops of yesteryear, but they were '*beyond cool*'. Dressed in smart, hip, casual suit jackets. John sat next to Joe, Paul to John's right, and the chat began.

Many years later I read how John Lennon described the night saying,

'*It was the most embarrassing thing I've ever been on.*'

This observation was the result of the questions asked. They were banal, weak and simplistic.

'*Will you ever be able to top Sgt. Pepper?*'

Irritating. How sad to have the two best songwriters in the world giving you twenty-two minutes of their valuable TV time, and you go '*light*'. So much that could be discovered, but so little was achieved. You are only as strong as your weakest link. In this case Joe Garagiola, and the NBC writers of the Tonight Show.

If you listen to the audio portion (the video portion is no longer available), it is truly cringe-worthy. Sitting with a slightly inebriated Tallulah Bankhead and a polite, but clueless, Joe Garagiola, John and Paul endured two eleven-minute segments of embarrassingly vacuous questions. A lost opportunity.

But not completely! The duo spoke to me. I felt it, heard it, understood the call. It connected with me clearly, personally, through the screen. I sat silent throughout the segments. On an island. My private place.

After an awkward introductory few minutes, John began the Apple pitch, his raison d'être. Paul looked on, in support of his mate. A friendship that was oak and bamboo, hand and glove, hello and goodbye. A continuous true partnership, which began the day that they joined forces on 6 July 1957. The afternoon that 16-year-old John met 15-year-old Paul at St. Peter's Woolton's Parish Church in Liverpool. The Quarrymen leader, John, had found his partner Paul at a church fete/garden party. The rough and ready Lennon and the smooth ambassador McCartney. A match made in heaven. They appeared to be extremely close, tight, that night. In his recognizable scouse drawl John explained,

"So, we've got this thing called 'Apple' which is going to be records, films, and electronics-- which all ties-up. And to make a sort of an umbrella so people who want to make films, and don't have to go on their knees in an office, you know, begging for a break. We'll try and do it like that. That's the idea. I mean, we'll find out what happens, but that's what we're trying to do."

As I recall, John and Paul invited any artist watching, to come to London. The famous Liverpudlian told me,

'Bring your songs, your poems, your books. No grey suited man will be waiting for you at Apple.'

The legendary composers had no guitars, they did not sing, they simply explained their Apple concept, then exited the stage. My mom always said it takes hours to prepare a meal, and within minutes its eaten. I had waited all day for this momentous occasion. In a flash, it was gone. I had recorded the audio on a cassette, which was lost in a move years later. Sad.

I was amazed at their maturity and their appearance. The two were now men, not boys. John was 27. Paul 25. They were no longer, *'Do You Want to Know a Secret,'* they were *'A Day in The Life.'* I saw two men that I respected. I heard two men speaking directly to me, offering me an opportunity, Apple Records.

Apple Records opened their doors in 1968. Founded as a division of Apple Corps Ltd. It was initially set up as a creative outlet for the Lads, plus other artists. Was it a success, yes. Was it a failure, yes. Even though Apple was declared the most successful new record company of the year for 1968, it soon became clear that the band members ignorance of finance and administration, combined with their naive utopian mission, had left Apple Corps with no solid business plan.

In the early years Apple Records released singles and albums by artists such as Mary Hopkin, Badfinger, Billy Preston, Jackie Lomax, and James Taylor. Most of these recordings were produced by The Beatles, and they even played on them now and then. So, the reason it had to be closed (though it remains as Apple Corps) must have been internal problems. The Beatles were not businesspeople. They were musicians. Today Apple Records is owned by Paul McCartney, Richard Starkey, Olivia Harrison, and Yoko Ono-Lennon.

What to do? I had $800 in savings in my Royal Bank Leo Savings-account. Money I had saved from working after school at Buy Low Foods as a grocery bagger. Money to pay my September 1968 university tuition. But I'm a dreamer. So, in July 1968, I flew BOAC to London with songs in my head, a smile on my face, and courage in my bag. I was off to see the Wizard, John Lennon, at Apple Records. The Shrine of the Holy. This was The Beatles after they had dropped *'Rubber Soul,'* *'Revolver'* and *'Pepper.'* Music that changed my life. What was I thinking? I was following my heart! Wonderful things come from courageous acts. Plus, I was invited.

London England. The Crown Jewels. The Thames. Tower Bridge.

Late afternoon and I had found a bed-sit room in Earls Court. A single bed, empty walls, literally it was five flights up. I dropped off my guitar and small knapsack and turned left and headed off to find Apple at 3 Saville Row.

Exhausted, jet lagged, and petrified by my own intention, I took two tube trains. Purchased a London street map. Asked a few questions of Londoners in the street, and voila 3 Saville Row. It was real. The stairs were there, as shown in the pictures I had seen. The Stairway to Heaven. A light meal on Earls Court Road, chicken a la king, and then I hit the sack. Big day tomorrow. Apple.

The next morning at 10am, focused and relaxed, I walked through the heavy front door with a #3 halfway up, on the right-hand wall, beside it. I went straight to the big oak reception desk. Three was always my lucky number.
 '*Hello,*' said the receptionist.
 She was my age, 17, friendly, smiling, and a Cockney. I smiled back,
 'Good morning, *my name is Barry Greenfield, and I've flown from Vancouver to meet John, to show him my songs!*' She seemed surprised.
 '*Do you have an appointment?*'
 'Sorry, no I don't' I replied. '*John was on TV, and he invited people to come to Apple with their music.*'
 A bit puzzled she asked, '*Can you take a seat please*'.
 On the floor behind her gigantic oak desk was a painting, not yet hung. It was still early days. It was the Apple logo. McCartney later explained that the big green apple logo was inspired by the Belgian surrealist painter Rene Magritte, an artist whose humour and ordinariness had captured his attention. There were two long church pews in the foyer near her desk. I sat on the pew facing the stairs. After about five minutes, up the stairs came John and Yoko.
 John was dressed in black, with a black hat on, Yoko in white, hatless.
 '*Hello Mr. Lennon,*' I said calmly and in awe. Smiling, he answered,
 '*Ello.*'
 Yoko was silent, a lot smaller, and three steps behind. He was dressed in the outfit he wore for the '*Hey Jude*' US LP cover. I could not breathe. Here was one of the reasons that I love music. Here was my lighthouse in the dark. John Lennon. I was in the same space as John Lennon. They walked into a large office to the left of the reception area.

I could hear them talking, and I could see John clearly. He removed his hat. His hair was long, and he was lanky. I sat there watching, listening, for 15 minutes. The odor of French Galois cigarettes permeated the air. Yoko and John were puffing away, the older man in a suit, sucked on a pipe. I was in a smoke-haze- dream and then............ a man in his mid-30's, Derek Taylor, the Apple's Publicist, approached me.

In early 1964, Brian Epstein hired Derek Taylor to run Beatles press releases and to act as the media liaison for the band and himself. Taylor resigned in September 1964, after a falling out with Epstein. In 1968 Taylor returned and was appointed head of publicity for The Beatles' Apple Corps. Between Beatle jobs he was the publicist for The Byrds, The Beach Boys and The Mamas and the Papas, in California. Derek Taylor was a key component in the Beatles Story, another Liverpublian to boot.

I shared my reasons for coming to London with Derek, who knelt down beside me. I stayed dead-still on the church pew.

'*Well John is rather busy today; can you leave him a cassette?*'

I explained that I had never recorded any songs and therefore did not have one. He asked me how I had planned to show the songs to John. I said,

'*On this.*'

I held up my acoustic, asleep in its case.

'*Oh! Well then.... will you play them for me?*'

'*OK, I'd love to!*'

We walked down corridor after corridor. Past room after empty room. We entered one. We both sat on the carpet (shag, I don't recall the colour, but it was well worn) and I pulled out my axe. I played Derek, '*Barry Songs*' from memory for 45 minutes with no lyrics, or papers.

'*You have amazing songs Barry. They're great. I love 'em. Let me talk to John. Please come back tomorrow at 10am*'.

I was back on Saville Row, alone in an empty street.
Back on the tube to Earls Court Station, I dropped my acoustic at the bed-sit, sat and thought for a bit then went out of the door and headed into London almost flying with joy.

The afternoon was spent at my favourite Gallery, the Tate, in the Henry Moore sculptures wing. I had lunch in a café, something and chips, then I walked along the Thames, glanced at Big Ben and The Houses of Parliament, then finally the peak stop of the day, Westminster Abbey. Then back to Earls Court. Chicken-a-la-king, again, in the same Earls Court Road café, and finally back to my tiny room. A shilling to use the communal-floor bathtub, ugh! They had no shower. I played my guitar, of course, then to my single bed, twelve hours before phase two at 3 Saville Row. Phase one running through my head, keeping me awake, reliving every moment of my exciting day at Apple, writing long passages in my journal. Was I dreaming? I had taken a giant leap, and I had cleared the bar.

I slept poorly. Up early, and back on the Tube. Inside the Apple door I found Derek Taylor waiting.

'Let's go, Barry.'

We walked through downtown London, and we talked about The Beatles, Canada, family, London, The Stones, and more until we arrived at the intended destination, EMI Headquarters, Manchester Square. I was about as nervous as a boy could be. I was in deep water. I was second guessing my decision to come to London. I hid it well. I knew that Derek and I had connected. It felt like he was on a mission for John.

Soon, I was standing in the spot where the *'Please Please Me'* LP cover was shot. I stood on the balcony railing forever enshrined on The Beatles inaugural LP, now ensconced in Hog's Hill, McCartney's home studio in Icklesham, East

Sussex by the river Brede. This is where The Beatles stood.

We went into a big corporate office, the office of Chris Webb, at Ardmore and Beechwood, the EMI Publishing House. He was waiting for us with tea, open arms, and warmth. He poured us a cuppa and smiled. Derek and Chris talked about ongoing business. I quietly listened and surveyed the simple office. Gold records, awards, some family photographs.

Chris was thirtyish, a Londoner, he was kind and seemed very experienced. Shoulder length hair. Educated. A southerner.

I always have had confidence in my songs. Fighting the ever-present jet lag, I was ready to share. I opened with '*Paint the World Greenfield.*' I sang six of the songs that I had shared with Derek.

We walked downstairs together. Into the bowels of the EMI complex. We arrived at a small studio, a control booth, and a recording room that was strewn with cables, microphone, baffles. It was real. I loved the feel. I had arrived. Larry Page, a manager, record producer, and record label owner waited for us.

Larry Page was the well-respected manager of The Kinks and The Troggs. He had worked on the Beatles 1964 tour that conquered America. I was in the midst of royalty. In truth, in 1968, I still struggled to tune my guitar, it was all new to me. Chris asked Larry, an established record producer, and label owner, Page One Records, to demo two of my songs, *'With This New Girl'* and *'Love is for the Young and Old.'* It was orderly and organized and I felt protected.

'These are two Barry Greenfield songs,' Chris Webb explained to Larry Page.

Then The Troggs arrived. Reg Presley, The Troggs song writer, and lead singer was talkative. He liked my *'Love is for the Young and Old'* song. The others looked bored, and in truth hungover. Larry suggested that his band would be a

good fit for me and my songs, suggesting that they play along with me, but I didn't feel it. I thanked him but I explained that I thought that the songs would be best served as written, on one guitar. At this point in my musical walk, I had never played with any other musician. I had no idea how.

I do not know where I found the courage to veto a dominating alpha like Page. Sometimes no is right. Following my heart is a habit that has served me well and still does. They all sat and watched as a I performed my two songs over and over until Larry Page was happy with the takes.

Larry Page showed little emotion as I worked. I sat on the EMI wooden stool in this foreign environment, never really sure if I was following his instructions correctly, which were minimal. Keeping my eyes closed, I just did what I did at home in my bedroom. Played the songs for me, listening as an audience of one. When I finished a take, Page simply said,

'Another'

I am unsure how many times I played each song, but I played for an hour, and I do believe I grew stronger.

We went back to Chris Webb's office on the Third Floor of EMI. Chris told me that he had spoken to John, on the telephone, earlier that morning, and had given him an update on my day. John wanted to record the two songs that we had demoed for Apple Records. I never was told the logistics of this plan. Who would be the producer? Who would play on the recording? Who would decide the arrangements? Instrumentation? Derek and Chris explained that Apple would release these songs as my first single. If it was received well, and charted, Apple would then produce a full LP of my original songs. *'Love is for the Young and Old'* would be the 'A' side. *'With this New Girl,'* the 'B'. It was all so tidy. But it was not what I expected. I had hoped that Apple or John, would say,

'*Great songs, a great singer would kill that one'*.

Derek, Chris, Larry and John, must have agreed that my voice was good enough to front the project. I had never sung in public. I had never sung in a choir. I had only sung at home. That day was my first experience with a real quality microphone, professional headphones, a crowd watching me, listening to me, judging. It was new. I am sure that Derek Taylor and Chris Webb believed that my songs were the key component. The hard part to find for any record label, and publisher is the song part. I was scared and overwhelmed by it all. Too much. Too quick.

I shuffled out of Manchester Square and walked to familiar turf, Piccadilly Circus. I called my mom from a pay phone on the street. You could call collect in 1968.

'*Mom, I saw John Lennon, and Apple like my songs.*'

I took photographs in a photo booth to commemorate the day. Then I went to Hyde Park, to think. To absorb what had happened in the last 48 hours. I walked the streets of London all day and well into the evening.

The night was weird. Surreal. I was 17 and alone in London. Afraid and extremely vulnerable. There was nobody close at hand that I trusted, to share this weight with. We all need to fly our ideas, available opportunities, and decisions by those that are in our orbit. I was part boy, morphing into part young man. My sister Suzan was not there. No trusted family or friend. I had bitten off a piece of the pie, and now, I had no idea what to do? Things had gone perfectly, but I had never thought it through. I just went. I had never exposed

my soul before that day or played my songs to strangers. I had never walked into an office, offered my songs, and asked,
 '*What do you think of these?*'
 I was so surprised at the acceptance, the speed of it all. I was weakened by the kryptonite that is the music business. Here I was in the final of the 100 metres at the Olympics, but I had never trained for the race. I had just run around the school track for fun. John Lennon, Derek Taylor, Chris Webb, and Larry Page were all sensitive and helpful. But I was simply not ready for this giant leap.

The next morning, I walked back to EMI at Manchester Square. An hour's walk from my bedsit. Unannounced, I walked into Chris Webb's office. I explained to him that I had never sung in public, barely knew what I was doing as a guitar player, and that my only reason that I came to Apple was to offer my songs to be used by other artist. Lennon and McCarney had done this for years, starting with the Stones, '*I Wanna Be Your Man*', Cilla Black, '*Step Into Love*', The Overlanders, '*Michelle*'. I saw myself as a Tin Pan Alley Writer. The fellow who composed and stayed off the stage. Cole Porter, Gerry Goffin, Hal David. Chris Webb listened intently, thought about who I was, and said,
 '*I understand Barry.*' He supported my conclusion.
 I believe Chris knew that the music business, Apple Records and the life that resulted from working in that industry, does not come without a cost.
 John Lennon's offer to me, to record my songs, and release a single on Apple Records, preceded the subsequent offers made to James Taylor, Jackie Lomax, Mary Hopkin and Badfinger. It was new ground for everyone involved.
 I came home to Vancouver.

I have thought for five decades about that decision. I have always seen fame as a poor win. True it brings money and adulation, but it has side effects. Trust, money management, insincerity and uncertainty about relationship choices.
 I love making music for arts sake. Was this decision right or wrong? Was I foolish, stupid? Was I fearful of success? Was I being smart? James Taylor suffered from depression. Two members

of Badfinger committed suicide. Its not all peaches and cream, a-la Paul McCartney.

In the years to come I would work with many greats. One can look back and wonder, but the only answer is to look at today. I am happy with all my journey. My music is still being born. New songs are always a delight to me. Music is an art, and selling it is not as important to me as creating it. My marriage, my family, my career, my 11 LPs on iTunes that sell globally (albeit like a gentle stream, that slowly meanders), my live gigs, my songs, my new found love for creating music videos, are the real story.

Both songs, chosen that Apple Day by Chris Webb, were recorded by Norrie Paramour, Cliff Richards orchestra leader, who was a huge name in the UK. I received SOCAN and PRO royalties, I used the money for university tuition.

I will never fully know John's plan. I assume he was trusting and respectful of Chris Webb and Derek Taylor, that wonderful Apple guy who shepherded me around London, and who knows maybe the receptionist told John I was polite? Plus, I had a Union Jack button on my army jacket. That never hurts.

George brought artists to Apple, Radha Krishna Temple, Jackie Lomax. Paul brought Mary Hopkin. Mal Evans and Peter Asher delivered Badfinger. To my knowledge John brought no one. Unless you want to include Barry Greenfield.

Footnote:
A part of me wishes I had said 'yes'. I would have lived the experience, and I would have known if I were able.

I do know that in 1968, I was not a good enough player, or capable singer. I had paid no dues at that point.

I will never know if passing on the Apple opportunity in 1968 was the correct decision. I am now five decades removed, and I am as unsure about that decision today as I was a week after I made it in 1968, sitting across from Chris Webb at EMI Headquarters in Manchester Square, London.

I do know that it was not a spontaneous call. I walked many miles, into the London night, with myself for company, thinking about the once in a lifetime offer from The Beatles HQ. I weighed the pros and the cons.

I knew that if I recorded the two tracks for John Lennon, there would be no guarantees.

James Taylor said 'yes', and he had a wonderful, rich career. An extremely talented man. But James was three years my senior, he had played professionally for many years prior to signing with Apple. He initially had a band, The Flying Machine. James talked in his biography about his difficulties with substance abuse. I also referred to Jackie Lomax, Jackie who? And the amazing Badfinger, produced by George Harrison and Paul McCartney, had two members, Pete Ham in 1975 and Tom Evans in 1983 who committed suicide. On a brighter note, Paul McCartney wisely guided Mary Hopkin.

'New York is Closed Tonight' was not a fluke. It was the most played song on Canadian Radio in 1972 and won the prestigious SOCAN Harold Moon Award for an outstanding contribution to Canadian Music. Like Lightfoot, Bachman, Mitchell, and Morissette did.

That award came three years after Apple. Three years of growth and hard work as a songwriter, singer, and guitarist. Feeding the root, exposing the soul. If I had walked through door #3, in 1968, and my songs had made the charts, it would have been a completely different life for Barry Greenfield. No regrets!

3

A Friday afternoon with Kenny Rogers in 1969

1969. I was eighteen. I was enjoying my first year at university, when independence called, *'Barry it's time to fly!'*. A tempting voice offering freedom and growth that we all hear from the shadows. Some choose to ignore it and remain safe and protected in their parents' home. Others follow this siren. I left the Birch Street apartment, our original Canadian family home. The apartment was nothing grand, a two-bedroom flat. I shared it with Mom, Dad, and sister Suzan. Suzan and I shared the smaller bedroom. Two twin beds and two sets of drawers. This is the room where I sat on my bed, and I first composed *'Barry songs.'* I learnt the tricks of the trade by studying and doing. Hour after hour, day after day. Talk minus action results in zero. Every song attempted is a brick in the songwriting wall.

I headed into the wild, into the hippie neighborhood of Kitsilano, Vancouver. My new digs were a rented top floor room, in a two-story communal house on Stephens and 2nd Ave, in the heart of Kits. This hippie/student locale existed as a ghetto for a generation in transit in 1969 Vancouver. I lived there for three years. Heaven. There were four other male *'roomies,'* who came and went, but I was the steady-eddy, and I ran the joint for the landlord. I had the best room; the kitchen worked; it had a clean bathroom and an OK shower. The house was run in a serious manner. I was strict with the assigned chores, and the place was comfortable, male-tidy, and relatively clean. Bliss. A straight ship that sailed right!

Rent was difficult to find. Being an English Literature student at Simon Fraser University meant hours of classroom attendance, reading, hard papers always due, and travel to and from on a slow bus, with frequent stops.

I knew that to survive, pay my tuition, and cover my rent and living expenses, I had to work. I made myself available for sixteen hours a week. Jobs came and went, grocery bagger; rental car employee; retail. All OK. All exhausting. All paid well.

Then one afternoon I struck gold. I was hired as a busboy at *'The Cave'*. A dream job, for me, at Vancouver's Premier Supper Club, located at 626 Hornby Street, in the heart of downtown Vancouver. Good pay, a solid dependable 21 hours a week, and brilliant live music every shift. I am always drawn to where music lives. Yabba dabba doo.

The world's finest entertainers were showcased at The Cave from 1937 to 1981. A partial list includes Louis Armstrong, Lenny Bruce, Duke Ellington, Ray Charles, Johnny Cash, Sonny and Cher, Diana Ross and the Supremes, the Everly Brothers, and a young Kenny Rogers and The First Edition in 1969.

Before becoming one of the 20th century's premier Country artists, and enjoying an iconic solo career, Kenny was the lead singer in a 6-piece pop Band, The First Edition. The band's style was difficult to classify. It incorporated elements of Country, Rock and even a taste of Psychedelic Pop, all done extremely well. Kenny managed the lead vocals and bass guitar and showed the world in this early incarnation how talented he truly was. It was obvious *'right out of the gate,'* Kenny Rogers had that illusive *'it-factor.'*

As the counterculture of the 1960s was developing, Kenny Rogers and The First Edition had their first big hit in early 1968, a psychedelic single. *'Just Dropped In, To See What Condition My Condition Was In.'* Then another smash hit *'But You Know I Love You,'* and once again in 1969, when they completed the trifecta with the topical *'Ruby, Don't Take Your Love to Town'*. A wonderful song about a disabled Vietnam veteran. A brave lyric. Unusual. Written by Mel Tillis.

These tracks were unique 45's and were all executed brilliantly. I learnt all the words, and I never changed my radio station when The First Edition was on. They were an American unit, not English, which added to their different feel, writing and approach. Not so much Kinks, but more Buffalo Springfield. They were a group yes, but Kenny stood out as the keyperson. Much like John Kaye of Steppenwolf, and in Creedence Clearwater Revival, where John Fogerty drove the bus.

I was studying five days a week at Simon Fraser University, with a career in Law in mind. Every Thursday, Friday and Saturday were my Cave busboy nights, and they were eagerly anticipated. I cleared tables, and I was a gopher for all the Cave Staff. But I got to listen to, and study, two sets of professional musicians nightly. Classroom in session. A dream gig for the music sponge Barry.

I arrived at the Cave's employee entrance at 6.30pm, headed home at 1.30am. The position lasted three months.

Any serving role in a busy restaurant is a non-stop ride. Delicate, focused, and exhausting. But I listened to the artists as I cleared. Glanced at the stage as I weaved between tables carrying a full, heavy tray of dirty dishes. I witnessed two sets a night. It was a busy and productive time. Sonny and Cher, The Temptations, The Fifth Dimension, Bobbie Gentry, and Kenny, plus more. I learnt a great deal from those hours in music university.

My life is marked by noticing an opportunity and acting on it. I watched The First Addition and I truly enjoyed their show. Kenny seemed approachable to me. I hatched a plan. I shared with no one about my intention to meet Kenny Rogers, I saw no need to idea that might not bear fruit. It was Friday noon on day two of Kenny's residency at the Cave. Arriving at 1pm, I walked up the staircase to the dressing room on the second floor. Armed with guitar and lyric book, as ready as any salesman at Brown Brothers preparing to sell a Ford, I knocked!

'*Come in*' he said.

The dressing room was small but crowded with decades of artifacts. A beat-up couch, two well used easy chairs. Randomly scattered clothing draped over the furniture. A guitar that I later discovered belonged to Kenny, a snare drum. Pictures adorned all four walls, capturing the long history of the club. It was perfect. A backstage set from a Humphrey Bogart and Lauren Bacall soundstage. A place lost in time, unchanged in twenty years. Kenny Rogers, age 30, sitting on that couch, bearded, big, smiling at me. In his Texan drawl he asked,

'*Who are you?*'

I had a routine. I employed it on Sonny and Cher, at the Georgia Hotel, Bobbie Gentry (in this very dressing room), and with The Fifth Dimension, in their Central Park Hotel near Hyde Park, and a few years earlier at Apple Records in London. I had my spiel rehearsed,

'Hello, I am Barry Greenfield, I'm a songwriter. I was hoping that you would listen to some of my songs and talk song writing with me?'.

Then I would shut up and wait. The thoughtful Texan smiled, thought for a second, understood, and said,

'*What you got Barry?*'

Krikey, it worked!

I pulled my guitar out of its case and began to tune it. I cannot actually recall the first song that I played but it was well received. I played him, '*With This New Girl,*' '*Paint the World Greenfield,*' '*Fireman at my Window,*' '*Roly Poly Ladies.*' He took the guitar from my young hands and showed me things that he suggested would strengthen and enhance them. He was right. I learnt about key changes that day. A trick I used countless times over the decades. Kenny Rogers taught me the simple, but extremely useful tool, the key change.

Soon we were talking music. What it meant. Its importance. Its relevance to understanding life. We agreed it was a beautiful gift to the soul.

Looking back, we were both so young. Me 18, Kenny 30. Here I am now 74, Kenny has passed. As I relive that day, or when I read my journal entry, and do my research about the man, I still feel the joy I felt in my heart being in the presence of a real professional. He was open and kind. He shared his experience and knowledge without fee, demand, or expectation.

I recall him explaining to me that he was a businessman who worked in music. A unique idea to me. He told me about the time that he spent with the New Christy Minstrels, in 1966, where he sang and played double bass. A valuable growing time in his musical walk. That he loved producing artists.

I would learn that it was Kenny who produced the early Don Henley recordings, with his Texan band, Shiloh. Rogers was born gifted. He cut his teeth producing Mickey Gilley and Eddy Arnold. Musical names that I knew from being a kid in Rhodesia/Zimbabwe listening to Country music. They played Country a great deal on the radio in Rhodesia/Zimbabwe and in South Africa. White men singing, not people of colour. It was subtle how they brainwashed the public. Better Jim Reeves than Little Richard. Better to give the kids Frank Ifield or The Andrew Sisters, than Joe Williams or The Platters.

For the next three hours, I was in class. He was happy to help the kid. Kenny discussed lyrics and melodies. He taught me about being honest, but mostly about being Barry. The best songs are real, the great songs are honest, memorable songs are truthful and thoughtful. If the person listening does not have a broken heart, but the singer can convey the feeling of a broken heart to the listener, then the listener will cry, as if that listener did have a broken heart. Deep but understandable when you are a songwriter.

Kenny helped me with my songwriting and confidence. He shared the tools that he had learned as a young student working with Eddy Arnold, and his years with the Minstrels. I had an open heart, and I was eager to be mentored. I learnt to ask nicely and listen when class was in session.

I may have not realized it on that day, but Kenny's gift is how he collaborated with people. This was evidenced by his partnerships with Dolly Parton, Lionel Ritchie, and Dottie West. He was inducted into the Country Music Hall of Fame in 2013. Rogers sold more than 100 million records worldwide during his lifetime, making him one of the best-selling artists of all time. He remade his career as one of the most successful cross-over artists ever.

The young Kenny Rogers that I shared an afternoon with was a revelation. He made me feel like I was not treading water, not wasting his time. He made me understand the value of songwriting, and the value of working hard on each lyric, each melody. I think of his version of *'Lady'* written by Lionel Ritchie in 1980. A song that is perfect in structure, emotion, and sentiment. Things Kenny found important.

'The idea was that Lionel would come from R&B and I'd come from country, and we'd meet somewhere in Pop'.

A few months ago, I recorded a Barry song *'Hanging on to You'*, a lyric and melody that arrived to show the love I felt for Lori. I followed the content, chapter, and verse, from Kenny's rule book for songwriting 101. He said:

'*Barry sing songs that are true. True stories, true words, and you will be OK.*'

I loved that gift. I have only written, and I only sing, and I only do, honest songs. The songs I compose are merely the journal of my journey.

I love my wife Lori, and the lyrics of '*Hanging on to You,*' simply and honestly state that fact. The truth is easily understood. I wrote:

>*I TIED A YELLOW BOW*
>*TO A BRANCH AROUND A TREE*
>*TO SHOW THE PEOPLE*
>*THAT WALK ON BY*
>*HOW MUCH YOU MEAN TO ME*
>*I DONT NEED A SHOOTING STAR*
>*TO FLY ME TO THE MOON*
>*I'M HANGING ON TO YOU.*

When a regular Joe meets someone famous, in the street, at a party, or in a dressing room, then the average person recalls the encounter for a lifetime, the celebrity not so much. '*Barry Tales*' are noteworthy events for Barry but are a mere blip for the protagonist. I imagine that our three-hour encounter vaporized for Kenny, much like Manchester fog disappears, but I can recall the place, the chat, the warmth to this day. Lucky me!

When I read that Kenny passed away on 20th May 2020, a Friday, I felt genuine sadness. We met on a Friday. He was eighty-one. I felt grateful that I had had the courage to knock.

He had announced a farewell tour in 2015 and was able to keep it going through December 2017. In April 2018, he announced that he was having to call off the remaining dates, due to unspecified health challenges. As he said:

'*I didn't want to take forever to retire*'.

He passed away peacefully at home from natural causes under the care of a hospice and surrounded by his family.

Here I sit in my studio. I can see the smiling face that sat on the beat-up Cave couch. Intense. Happy. Loving the role of teacher and wise owl.

Footnote

My encounters, over the years, have altered the trajectory of my journey in music. The positive meetings, Sonny and Cher, Apple Records, John Lee Hooker et.al., always resulted in confidence and personal growth. If I had to have one 'tale' that affected me the most, it would be the afternoon I spent with Kenny Rogers in 1969.

They are all important, all life changing, but Kenny Rogers was a giant leap for me. He was special.

We shared three hours together in a small dressing room upstairs in The Cave. He was new to fame; it still had a lower case 'f.' The stellar accolades were yet to arrive.

I was blessed to be allowed to sit in a room with a natural.

As Paul McCartney wrote, 'in the end the love you take, is equal to the love you make.'

4

The day Cher kissed me (on the cheek) 1970

A new decade had arrived, welcome to the seventies. I was now a university student working at the Cave nightclub, three nights a week. I could pay my tuition, my rent, buy food and sundries. The Cave, Vancouver's premier supper club dreamed it was like a showroom in Vegas North, but in truth it was more like Reno Central. There is nothing wrong with that.

The range of performers that graced the Cave's stage was interesting and diverse. During my tenure I witnessed the 5th Dimension, Bobby Gentry, Kenny Rogers and The First Edition, Mitzi Gaynor, The Ink Spots, Sonny and Cher and more.

My job was to be the world best busboy. My shift began at 7pm and ended with me collapsing exhausted on the Fourth Avenue bus heading home at 1.30am. Thursday through Saturday.

I have had many student hires, but I worked my tail off at this one. Collecting plates and dishes, filling up a big tray, and then trying to carry them safely to the kitchen without incident. Spreading out a new white tablecloth on a round table, then putting the place settings on correctly. It took a bit, but I mastered it. To the best of my recollection, not one tray dropped enroute.

I was constantly hungry, delivering tempting main courses to the middle-aged, middle-class, couples. I watched them slowly, and inevitably, get inebriated. I can only imagine how many drove how swell over the limit. Life in the seventies. A haze of cigarette smoke sat like a cloud above the room. *'Yes Sir, No ma'am, three bags full.'* The Cave used minimum staff, so we all had to be beavers, or we would be let go by management.

But I witnessed two-solid-musical-sets a night, of world class performers. Ears and eyes wide-open.

My pay was slightly above minimum wage, $1.85 an hour, plus a small share of the evening's tips. I got home, watched late TV, and then met Morpheus the son of Somnus at sunrise.

Throughout my Cave tenure, I looked for opportunity to showcase my songs. My goal was to share with the performers the fact that I was a fledgling songwriter, and that I wanted to learn. I had to be courageous, and I needed to be proactive. One weekend the most famous duo in showbiz, Sonny and Cher, were at the Cave, all three of my working nights. A chance to walk through door number two. What was required was some solid Lieutenant Colombo-like detective work, *so* I asked my friend Kevin, the Cave's doorman,

'Which hotel are they staying at Kevin?'

Sonny and Cher were staying at the posh Rosewood Hotel Georgia, a short block and a half south. It was a beautiful Vancouver landmark. I phoned the front desk of the Rosewood Hotel Georgia, at noon, September 19th, 1970, a Saturday.

'Sonny Bono's room please?'

I was immediately connected. Security was not as it is today, and one could actually get through on a telephone. A few years later I called Sheryl Crow on her hotel room phone. Front desk connected me. That would not happen today.

'Hello,' answered a female voice.

I was thrilled to get through, but I wondered to myself, is this Cher?

'Good morning, my name is Barry Greenfield, I am a local songwriter, and I would love to play my songs for you and Sonny. I have one song that I think you can use?'

Silence. Then the lady with the kind voice handed the receiver to Sonny. His

recognizable nasal drone was evident.

He was laughing at my request. He asked how I found them. I was honest and mentioned Kevin, and the fact that I was a busboy at the Cave who wanted to be a songwriter. He immediately said,

'Ok, let's meet at 2pm, we're in room 809.'

I was gobsmacked. Whenever I am direct, use a calm voice, express myself clearly, I seem to arrive at affirmative.

The Rosewood Hotel Georgia is a 12-story historic hotel located at 801 West Georgia Street in the city core. It opened its magnificent doors in 1927. It is a bit of New York, and a lot of Vancouver. Brick and wood.

I arrived early. I sat in the lobby on an oversized armchair until my Bar mitzvah watch read 1.55pm. Walking into the lift, pushed eight, and I headed to room 809. I was lucky to be early, as I could reset, and gather my thoughts. The Rosewood Hotel Georgia was a luxury hotel with big hallways, paintings on the walls, solid doors, and flowers by the elevator.

Big deep breath, a quick check of my appearance, I knocked. Cher opened the door. Dressed in jeans and an expensive, rainbow, silk blouse. Hair long, black, and down. She was smiling.

'Hello, you must be Barry?'

'Yes, thank you so much for seeing me.' I walked in, and I stood there, numb, frozen, overwhelmed by where I was standing, and whom I was two feet from, Cher.

Cher was so striking, so familiar. I recalled when I was a yard away from John Lennon in Apple Records in 1968 that it felt identical. I knew that they
were both human, but not human like my mates at school. Its me who went weird, not Cher, she was relaxed and warm to me, normal, natural.

The room was not a suite. But it was a large space, with a king-sized bed, a couch, a desk, suitcases, clothes, some dirty room service dishes, and ever-present daily life things. It looked a lot like the hotel room I now share with my wife Lori, on our holidays, except ours is tidier. Sonny walked towards me, we shook hands and smiled. All a bit uneasy. Then both Cher and Sonny sat on the king bed, waiting for *Barry's pitch.*

I had experience showcasing my songs for 10cc, Apple Records, The Troggs. I was not in awe, but respectful, and appreciative. In fact, I remember being confident.

'So, Barry,' began Sonny. *'No one has ever asked us to do this before.'*

I made solid, direct, eye contact with him. I replied that my goal in life was to be a songwriter like him, Harrison, Mitchell, and Webb. To accomplish that I needed to be brave, and that I acted if opportunity presented itself. I told them that being a busboy at The

Cave offered me a superb vantage point to watch great artists and learn. I spoke with sincerity and candour. I shared that I loved their show. The music, the humour, the spark when Cher laughed. Cher found that amusing. I thought their set was smooth, entertaining and fun. *'I Got You Babe'*, and *'The Beat Goes On'*, were two that I stopped to watch from the back of the room. Sonny said thank you. The ingredients needed for the soup of success are, equal parts courage, self belief, humility and truth.

Sonny made me feel more relaxed. He spoke of his early days as a songwriter and how he learnt from the legendary Phil Spector, adding that he agreed, courage is supreme. I was honoured to have him talk about his early years with me. His story fascinated.

He met Cher in 1962 at an LA coffee shop. Sonny was working for record producer Phil Spector at the famous Gold Star Studios. Through Sonny, Cher started as a session singer, and sang backup on several of Spector's classic recordings, including *'Be My Baby'* by The Ronettes, and *'You've Lost that Loving Feeling'* by The Righteous Brothers. A wonderful history.

Getting connected with Sonny was easy. Sonny was friendly and open. Cher was present but silent. She moved off the bed and sat in the large armchair. Waiting!

Then Sonny said, 'What do you want to play us?'

I began my mini concert. Sitting on a chair in front of the dresser, I played the couple six songs. Sonny talked about one especially, *'I've Never Been This Happy Before.'* He brought out his tape recorder and asked me to play it again. He taped it, and Cher sang along, intermittently, quietly in the chorus. I was thrilled. They both seemed to think it had possibilities. Sonny wrote down my name and home phone number. I never heard anything more from him. My father instilled in me that the important thing is to try. I had tried.

How many times in my journey had I had excitement over a song, to see it result in a promise to do something that never reached fruition? I do not think its because people say what you want to hear. I imagine its because life moves on, and the idea of *'I've Never Been This Happy Before'* fades like a candle that flickers and goes out. It may have ended differently if I could have followed up with a telephone call to Sonny a week after our meeting, but I did not.

A classic example of how one gets an act to do one of your songs is.

'*I Wanna Be Your Man*' the Stone's second single in 1963, which reached number 12 in the UK. The song was finished by McCartney and Lennon in the corner of a club in front of Jagger and Richards. The boys from Liverpool saw a chance and took it.

Mick Jagger recalled *I Wanna Be Your Man's* genesis in an interview in 1968:

'We knew [the Beatles] by then, and we were rehearsing, and Andrew (the Stones manager) brought Paul and John down to the rehearsal. They said they had this tune; they were really hustlers then. I mean, the way they used to hustle tunes was great: 'Hey Mick, we've got this great song.' So, they played it, and we thought it sounded pretty commercial, which is what we were looking for, so we did it like Elmore James or something. I haven't heard it for ages, but it must be pretty freaky because nobody really produced it. It was completely crackers, but it was a hit and sounded great onstage.'

The three of us, Cher, Sonny and me, chatted a bit more. About personal things, travel, my family, and then Cher stood up, animated for the first time,

'Barry lets go for a walk. Show us a bit of Vancouver please.'

It was the second time that she had used my name. I may have blushed.

I had been in the room for over an hour, where it was all about Sonny, he was doing business. I occasionally glanced at Cher, hoping I was not busted!

Cher was 24, Sonny 35. He seemed more like her dad than her fella. She seemed a little sad. Beautiful to a fault, even more so than her pictures. Sonny was my height, five foot six, Cher maybe an inch taller. Both wore sneakers and were dressed expensively. Sonny laughed a lot, Cher was serious. That was about to change.

I left my guitar with the doorman and we were outside the Hotel on Vancouver's busiest downtown thoroughfare, Georgia Street. We turned right and walked towards Vancouver's famous Stanley Park, in the northwestern half of Downtown. Many years later, in 2014, Stanley Park was named *'top park in the entire world'* by TripAdvisor based on reviews submitted. I was proud to share the beauty of my home town with my two guests.

Cher walked beside me; Sonny stopped a lot to gaze into shop windows. He stopped at a high-end men's shoe store, but he did not go in. Cher looked happy to be out in the fresh air. It was a lovely day in Vancouver, and it was unusually quiet on Georgia street. It was 1970 and *the village of Vancouver* was still manageable as a City.

After twenty minutes we found ourselves at the corner of Cardero and Georgia, at the Beauchant Mowatt Gallery. A lovely art gallery, one of Vancouvers best. Cher had talked and walked alongside me the entire 20 minutes. She peppered me with questions about Vancouver, my family, what music I listened to, good local shopping areas. I told her about *Robsonstrasse,* the hip shopping area. I asked her questions about her records. She thanked me for my kind words. She told me that she was getting better at singing. I told her I was not. She laughed and complimented my singing in the room. We truly connected. She was young, like me. It was fun. I developed a crush, who wouldn't. To this day I am most comfortable with strong independent women, like Lori.

We entered the gallery. Silently we walked through the ground floor. Nothing seemed to resonate with either of them, or me, so we left quickly. We crossed the street to the south side and walked sloth-slow back to the hotel.

To my surprise no one seemed to notice or recognize my famous walking partners. To me they looked just like Sonny and Cher, yet, who would expect to see them, there? I recall a few years ago, drinking coffee, sitting in a Starbucks window seat, staring at Neil Young, who was in the street less than three yards from me talking to someone for ten minutes. He was wearing his iconic fringe jacket. No one looked twice at him. He was, like my famous duo, invisible.

The walk back was a little quieter. Cher seemed happy to be a *'free-man-in Paris'*, Sonny was enjoying the slow gait. They did not chat. Cher occasionally remarked how nice my city was. She seemed at peace with the quiet, the freedom, and simply taking a walk.

It was 5pm and we were back at the hotel entrance. I opened the heavy glass door for Cher. She smiled, turned to her husband and said, '*Why aren't you more of a gentleman, like Barry?*'

Then it happened. **She leaned towards me and kissed me on the cheek.** Was I surprised, was I taken aback? A little, but it felt appropriate, and kind. She was saying thank you for being normal. I saw the three of us having a bond of music. Sonny shook my hand. They bade me farewell and were gone.

That tender moment was my validation that the afternoon was real. I recall the day with a great deal of fondness. Both of these world-famous entertainers were decent, nice and open to life. I had lucked-out. Its great when you take a chance, and the reward is paid.

I retrieved my acoustic, and headed to the bus stop to ride home.

As I have lived through the next five decades of my life, I have always paid attention when their names would come up. Newspapers. TV. Movies. Magazines and the like. I followed Sonny the mayor, the politician, and Cher the icon. I assume that they both got what they wanted. Finding the balance between ultra fame, and day to day life, is difficult, I imagine.

Last week I watched Taylor Swift's Eras tour video. She and Cher are in a similar place in this material world. *Nothing is real.* The screaming, the noise, the instant recognition, the demands. The constant security. The ever-present and intrusive media eyes. *Strawberry Fields Forever*! Cher has lived it all her adult life. Her personal relationships are scrutinized. It is a cage that megastars are protected by and yet frustrated by too.

I look back at my three hours with them with a bit of wonder. They had not arrived at the destination, or heights, which was to come. I sensed that they both knew that the stars had aligned, and that they were on a grand tour to fame and fortune. Sonny just seemed to be at work. Cher seemed most happy when she was simply being Cherilyn Sarkisian.

Footnote:

I think that what I recognized in that hotel room was correct. A controlling man and his prize jewel? During 1974 in divorce proceedings, Cher cited 'involuntary servitude' as the reason for the pair's split. The legal proceedings turned sour as she accused Sonny of withholding her rightful earnings. Love sometimes is a nail and money sometimes a hammer.

I loved the few hours that I spent with Cher and Sonny. The two stars in waiting were still holding onto normal. They were sleeping in a standard hotel room not a presidential hotel suite. They worked at The Cave, in front of 150, not the LA Forum in front of 17,500. I shared time with two nice people. I put another brick in the wall.

There was never a word from Sonny Bono about my song. I thought that the experience was so warm and special that I never felt regret. I was overjoyed that I had a chance to share a few hours, with the world's biggest duo.

Cher's two-part memoir came out in November 2024. I doubt she has a chapter titled 'The day I kissed Barry Greenfield (on the cheek) in 1970'. But she did! Such is life in the real world.

5

10cc, 'Sweet America' my first recording, Stockport 1971

Manchester Autumn 1971. I am travelling solo, upstairs, in a double-decker, the number 59 bus. My much loved, six-string acoustic guitar sits next to me, a passenger too. The bus, is green, which is unusual, as most English buses are red. The route, straight down Cheetham Hill Road. I jump on in Higher Crumpsall. In the North End of England's second City. I was born in Crumpsall Hospital, nineteen years earlier and I spent my first seven years as a Mancunian. To this day that is who, and what I am, a Manchester man. My father was true Manchester City blue, me I am simply red. United.

I was nineteen, and I had returned to my birthplace to chase a rainbow and jump into the fire. I needed to know, and I wanted to see, if I would be accepted as a songwriter. The trip to London and Apple Records in 1968, was in my rear view mirror, but the words of John Lennon and Chris Webb, at Ardmore and Beechwood Publishing, reverberated in my ears.

'Lets record two songs and see what transpires. If they are liked, we will record an LP of your songs for Apple Records'.

I could not erase the thought,

'what if I had said yes?'

It mattered not, I was not ready, then, but now, I had grown, I felt more in control, and I was better prepared for the challenge. I had played a bit live, I had sung with a few other musicians, not a lot, but a few times. I felt like a songwriter, not a guitarist. I still do. My thinking was that the second city, Manchester, would be less invaded by musicians hawking their wares than London. As we all flog our art to the music-suits.

I recall being immersed with one song that week in England, the one hit wonder by Thunderclap Newman, *'Something in the Air.'*

The song had wormed its way into my consciousness. I could not lose that lyric,

'Call out the instigators, because there's something in the air, we got to get together sooner or later, because the revolution's here'.

So catchy. Quality production by my favourite guitarist Pete Townsend. A song well written by Speedy Keen and originally titled *'Revolution'*, but Townsend changed it because of Lennon's song. I love it to this day. Maybe that lyric lingered because there was *something in the air*?

With Thunderclap running through my head I had a plan, to visit Manchester music publishers. I had the addresses written in my book. Locations that I researched in the Manchester telephone directory. Deansgate, central Manchester, here I come.

Grey coat, black gloves, and a warm red heart, I looked around at my fellow travellers, bus-neighbours. I saw row after row of empty seats, then my eyes land on a girl my age, she was sitting alone in the front row. Never being afraid to chat, and believing a kind word is well received, I moved ahead to talk to her. Her name was Bernice Seger. Trust is a trait easily found in England's friendly North. She saw my acoustic guitar bag.

'Are you a musician?' *'No, I'm a songwriter.'*

To my amazement she told me that her boyfriend was Lol Crème. Crème was a member of Hotlegs, a trio that had recorded *'Neanderthal Man.'*

'Neanderthal Man' was initially created only as a studio exercise to test drum sounds on new recording equipment, but it sold over two million copies and reached No. 2 in the UK in August 1970. Truth is stranger than fiction! Bernice pulled out a piece of paper from her purse and wrote down Lol Crème's telephone number. In time, and down the road the band, Hotlegs, Lol Crème, Eric Stewart and Kevin Godly would add Graham Gouldman, on bass, and morph into the English gem, 10cc.

The day in Deansgate visiting publishers was fruitless. I got nowhere. But all was not lost, I had a telephone number to call when I got back to Aunt Sadie's and Uncle Bert's house on Cedric Road. Lol Crème.

They had a rule in their home. A shilling per call. I put a shilling on the kitchen counter and dialed. I talked too fast. I tend to do that when nervous. I shared my story with Lol, about the number 59 bus, and my meeting with Bernice, and that I had flown from Canada to meet publishers in Manchester. Crème was testy, smug, and a wee-bit unfriendly. He clearly did not appreciate this type of intrusion, and he had no desire to help me with guidance, and/or mentorship. Frustrated, his answer was rushed,

'*Call my business manager, that's his job, not mine.*'

He gave me Harvey Lisberg's, telephone number, then hung up. I was extremely grateful. What a gift. Lisberg's personal home number. I had struck gold. Thanks, Lol.

Lisberg was the manager of Herman's Hermits, Freddie, and the Dreamers, Hotlegs/10cc, Andrew Lloyd Webber, Tim Rice and more. He was the marketer behind '*Mrs Brown You Have a Lovely Daughter,*' '*I'm Telling You Now,*' '*Henry the Eighth*' and Andrew Lloyd Webber. In 1969 Andrew arrived at great acclaim with '*Joseph and the Amazing Technicolour Dreamcoat*', wonderful lyrics written by Tim Rice. Lisberg was a major player in the UK Music Scene. I had access to a gigantic fish in the big UK pond. The universe smiled at me that day. Thank you Bernice, appreciated Lol.

Sitting in Aunt Sadie's tiny kitchen on one of the two wooden chairs, at the small table, I dialed Lisberg. Another shilling. He answered with an educated sounding voice. not street Mancunian. I mentioned Lol, '*Neanderthal Man,*' songwriting, and my intention. Without hesitation, he invited me to walk the twenty-five minutes to visit him at his home. I immediately headed out the door to my destiny, with guitar in hand. Same grey coat, same black gloves and a rapidly beating red heart pounding in my 19-year-old chest.

The house loomed large. It was posh, in an upper-class, Manchester, neighbourhood. It was difficult to conceive that it was within walking distance of Aunt Sadie's small semi-detached, working-class street.

People with money never unhinged me. I was certainly working-class north of England and made my own way. We lived modestly, dressed appropriately, had some toys, but lacked little. Safe, warm, and loved.

'Ding Dong,' he answered. A round, balding man, seasoned, 30, but looked older, greeted me.

'Barry? Come in, lets go to my den.'

A lovely vibe filled the well-appointed home. I was not used to expensive art, ornate vases, glass sculptures. Carole Lisberg came to check out the stranger. I doubt Harvey met many song peddlers in his private place, and I would discover that he had large, well staffed offices in Manchester. Many music divisions. Even in his home he was not casual in any sense of the word. All business. White collared shirt, dark suit pants, polished leather laced Oxford shoes. A man who flew his flag. A man of wealth.

I sensed that Carole was doing her due diligence, protecting Harvey from a potential invader. She questioned my intentions, and I must have passed her litmus test. We became very close over time, and in fact Carole Lisberg became my champion in many ways. She was not a shrinking violet. Carole expressed her admiration for both *'Sweet America'* and *'Dorothy's Daughter',* the two songs that cemented my relationship with Lisberg. I played them for her many times on my acoustic when visiting them. Carole was very kind and extremely supportive. Behind every great man stands a strong woman.

Lisberg's career began in 1963 as a trainee accountant. His introduction to music was when he discovered Herman's Hermits in 1963 at a church hall in Davyhulme an area of Urmston in Greater Manchester.

I sat on an ottoman. He sat on his throne. I played him two verses and a chorus of *'With This New Girl,'* the Barry Greenfield song that Apple Records picked as my 'A' side in 1968. Harvey stopped me. Without leaving his seat he picked up the black telephone and dialed Graham Gouldman.

'Graham, I have this kid here who's great, sounds like Cat Stevens.' (I had never heard of Cat Stevens). Gouldman was about to leave with his wife Susan for Ringway Airport, and Mallorca, on holiday.

'Can you stop by, on the way to Ringway, and give a listen?'

The English *wunderkind* Graham Gouldman, then 24, was a Barry Greenfield songwriting hero. His catalogue helped shape my early songwriting and focus. Unusual lyrics, catchy tunes, great song titles. I understood as a young writer the importance of the title. Some interesting titles that shaped my thinking were *'A Whiter Shade of Pale'* by Gary Brooker, Mathew Fisher, and Keith Reid; *'Paperback Writer'* by Paul McCartney, and the title that I *borrowed* from an advertisement in Life magazine about electricity, *'New York is Closed Tonight'*. Strong. Unique. Eye catching titles.

I had known of Gouldman's skill since early 1964. He had written two early Hollie monsters, *'Bus Stop'* and *'Look Through Any Window'*. I was living in Manchester in the early sixties. That is when I fell in love with music. The Kinks, The Hollies, The Beatles, The Dave Clark Five. They became my family. The connection made in 1963 and 1964 is solid to this day. British Pop at its finest. I returned to Africa in 1965.

In an unusual twist of fate, the first song I learnt at age 15, was *'For Your Love'*, another Gouldman composition. It was recorded by The Yardbirds. There are no accidents. I later shared this fact with Graham. It fell on deaf ears; Graham was not sentimental.

A half dozen *songs* later, Gouldman walked in. Dressed to the nines in an expensive heavy winter coat, wool-scarf, cool and musical. Susan Bloom, 22, Graham's wife, and soon to become a dear friend of mine, strolled in with him, two steps in front. They had a vibe. Wealth. Money. Success. Out of Vogue, a magazine power couple, photo spread. Early *'Bennifer'* vibe. His energy was 100% rock star. On top of the world. Confident. I was intimidated, and for the first time I felt out of my depth. No time for that, it was time to work.

Susan and Carole, who I later discovered where sisters, slipped off into the huge, by UK standards, kitchen. Graham, Harvey, and I returned to the den. I picked up my acoustic. I took a deep breath and played a song for one of my heroes. A chance to share my wares with one of the most iconic British songwriters and his manager.

I played three songs. My strongest three. Harvey spoke frequently throughout. Mentioning things, he liked about my work, and questioned Graham about content, and hooks.

'Nice,' was all that Graham said. It was sincere. All business. The brief 20-minute visit was ending. Mallorca and Ringway Airport were calling. Gouldman stood for the entire performance,

He did not remove his coat or scarf. His decision was immediate. Looking directly at Harvey he said,

'Let's record Barry when I get back.'

He then turned to me to share the plan.

'Barry, write a single. When I get back, we will pick the strongest candidate. Then we will go into Strawberry and make a hit.'

Was I dreaming? It was an experience that I can recall with clarity to this day. I was in the room with a famous writer. I played my songs for him. He was positive. He wanted to work with me.

Lisberg had managed Gouldman for years. I was surprised to learn that the lyrics, which shaped me, *'No Milk Today,' 'Bus Stop,' 'Evil Hearted You'* were actually from the pen of Graham's father, Hymie, a playwriter of some note in the Manchester area.

To this day Graham Gouldman is the finest songwriter with which I have shared a room. He taught me a great deal. I found a mentor that fit my style perfectly. I have written songs with Graham over the ensuing years. Some recorded. Some did not. One or two are special ones.

I asked Harvey to explain what Graham had in mind with his closing salvo *'we'll go into 'Strawberry'.*

Strawberry North is the recording studio in Stockport, where I cut my teeth and was *baptized* as a professional musician. The music room is a piece of UK music history. I feel blessed to have worked there in its infancy.

Let me explain why the idea of Strawberry arrived in 1968, and the reason it was successful.

'In September 1962, the quartet from Liverpool, The Beatles, recorded *'Love Me Do'* in EMI Studios in London. The enormous world changing British Invasion was about to begin. Most of the recordings, by these brilliant British bands, were done in London.

The Animals came from Newcastle upon Tyne and recorded their early hit, *'House of the Rising Sun,'* in the Capital. The Zombies were formed in St. Albans, and they tracked *'She's Not There'* in London. Most of the music that was born in the North, in the Midlands, Wales, or Scotland was put to tape in the south of England. There was a plethora of Recording Studios in London;

Trident, Gooseberry Sound, Abbey Road, Olympic to name but a few.

In Manchester, Peter Tattersall, the road manager of Billy J. Kramer and the Dakotas, *'Little Children'*, and Eric Stewart, guitarist, singer, in The Mindbenders, *'A Groovy Kind of Love'*, conceived a gold idea. *'Let's open a studio in the North. The need is obvious, and it will save travel, and costs incurred by bands closer to our base camp'.* Strawberry North was built in Stockport a few short miles outside the thriving, and growing, Manchester metropolis.

Soon 10cc, Gouldman, Stewart, Godley, and Crème, moved in, and made it the Bands home-base. They purchased great gear, incorporated intelligent and sound architecture, and created a wonderful facility. Strawberry became a legendary place to make records.

From 1968 to 1990, the room was used by 10cc to create, write, and record their albums. '10cc', 'Sheet Music', 'The Original Soundtrack'. Paul, Linda, Mike McCartney, The Stone Roses, The Smiths, The Moody Blues and even Cliff Richard came through the front door. The name 'Strawberry' came from Eric Stewart's favourite Beatles song, *'Strawberry Fields Forever'*.

I did not linger luxuriating in my opportunity to work with Gouldman. I had work to do. Graham's directive was clear, *'Write a single, wrote a hit'.* A task that was new to me, challenging, but one that I did not find daunting. I considered the word *'hit'*. I assumed, it should be three minutes in length, it should contain two verses, a chorus, then repeat the first verse, do the chorus twice and then fade-out. Make it catchy, be repetitive, and be radio friendly. I never considered danceable, as that was not my forte.

I had never thought about writing a radio song before. I wrote songs that I knew and felt, that told my story, exposed my soul. But if Mark Bakan could write *'Pretty Flamingo'* for Manfred Mann, and Tony Hatch could sculpture *'Downtown'* for Petula Clark, I could emulate that. It's a formula.

The next morning Aunt Sadie was at Aunt Betty's and Uncle Bert was at the factory, leaving me alone in the house. I began the task ahead. Much like a school exercise that I completed the night before it was due. I sat in the Centre of Aunt Sadie's couch, guitar in hand, paper and pencil ready. In situ I suddenly decided to change track. I felt like composing a non-radio song. It was a conscious decision. I did not want to sing a catchy poppy tune. I would struggle to compose a great song like *'My Boy Lollipop'*, written in the mid-fifties by Robert Spencer, and popularized, a radio staple in 1964, by Millie Small. I wanted to offer Graham my art. Being honest to who I was as a writer, not motivated by commercial desire.

I began to think about Vietnam. I listen to my heart when writing a song. Frequently I start a piece, and it ends up in a different place than I imagined. The media of the day was focused on the conflict in Vietnam. The US continued unilateral withdrawal of force from South Vietnam. TV, newspapers, Time magazine, were overflowing with the slow ending South Asian war.

An idea arrived. It's as clear to me today as it was that afternoon in Manchester. It would be titled *'Suite: America'*. The goal, to write a three-part song in the mold of the 1969's epic *'Suite Judy Blue Eyes'*, by Stephen Stills. Three distinct and separate ideas. One 7-minute song. It was an interesting challenge.

I began with verse one,
'I think it's time I moved from Oklahoma, there's 49 more ways to live my life,'.

Draft dodgers had been leaving the US in droves, I had met many in Vancouver's fourth Avenue scene. A neighbourhood where hippies congregated. I had the opening couplet. I quickly completed the verse, I arrived at the point that would suit the song's chorus, naturally, effortlessly. I sang *'Sweet America, eulogize America, then fall down on your knees and cry'*. To me it summed up the war precisely, honestly, and accurately, *'America, fall down on your knees and cry'*.

I wrote the entire song in 20 minutes. No longer a trilogy, but now a single, focused, clear thought. An anti-war song. I had no idea if I had a hit for Gouldman, but it was a Barry song. This song has been recorded by eight different acts (that I am aware of), in my career. Six nailed it, two did not get it at all.

Protest Music has been a musical vehicle for awareness for over 200 years. Music to think about. Dylan gave us *'Blowing in the Wind'*; Donovan sang *'Susan on the West Coast Waiting'*; Lennon wrote his powerful '*Revolution*'; PF Sloan and Barry McGuire, inspired with '*Eve of Destruction*'. '*Sweet America*' was cut from the same cloth.

Neil Young said that it is easier for Canadians to write about America because Canadians sit outside the fishbowl, and we look into it. He wrote '*Southern Man*', '*Ohio*'. Saskatoon's Joni Michell composed '*California*'. Gordon Lightfoot gave us '*Black Day in July*'.

Graham returned from Mallorca and he drove to Aunt Sadie's within hours of arriving home, to review my work. Exam papers being marked. All the neighbours were peeping out of their front-room windows, astonished by the gleaming silver Aston Martin in front of Aunt Sadie's'. An unpredictable sight. Work vans and clunkers were the general vehicles on view on Cedric Road. My neighbours were bus people, only a few owned cars. James Bond was in town. I had three songs ready to submit. I was nervous, worried, and unconfident. He was Graham Gouldman.

Gouldman liked all three. He was most happy with '*Sweet America*'.

'*We got a hit Barry!*'

In fact, the second one I played for him, '*The Joker*' was recorded by Garden Odyssey, a band he produced at Strawberry. It charted in the UK. Now a forgotten fragment of Greenfield history. If it were asked on *Jeopardy* no one would buzz in.

Three days later the same 'Bondmobile' pulled up at noon. We drove to Stockport and chatted all the way to Strawberry North. The studio's street location sat in a neighbourhood where one should buy apples and tea towels, not make hits. But as soon as we walked inside, it felt great. It was small, but compact. Eric Stewart at the mixing console, Lol Crème tuning his brown Gibson, and Kevin Godley smiling at me, all waiting to work. Handshakes and off we go.

Graham played bass, lead guitar, and produced. Kevin on the kit, Lol on rhythm, Eric on the board, with Peter Tattersall alongside. I sang. They all worked well together and seemed happy to follow Graham's instructions.

'*Sweet America*' was easy to get right. I had a strong understanding of tempo, breaks, and the arrangement required. Graham had thought his part through too. '*Fuzz lead guitar, two acoustics, basic Kevin on the kit, no piano, three-part harmony on the chorus. Barry vocal front and centre. Doubled.*' But unfortunately, in the final playback the track felt a bit muddy, lacked subtlety. My thinking was that they were the experienced men in the room, their vision was preferred. It was my first studio experience, at this level, I was petrified going in and now '*Sweet America*' was complete. Amen. Eight hours. Mixing came later, plus a few overdubs and a small number of fixes.

I felt an enormous sense of accomplishment. I had written a song on demand, thought through an acceptable arrangement, practiced it over a hundred times, and now it was recorded with the help and support of this soon to be historic unit, 10cc, the quartet that gave the world, '*I'm Not in Love*'. It was a milestone for Barry. What I dreamt could happen, had happened. What added to my satisfaction, was that the song talked to the sad state of global affairs in 1971, the ongoing conflict in Vietnam. It was a song with thought. The message I intended was understood. It was not as big a message as Dylan's '*Masters of War,*' but I saw '*Sweet America*' as its distant cousin.

'*Sweet America*' is still a staple of my live set, and it remains one of my most audience requested songs. Be it Vietnam, Watergate, Mission Accomplished, Desert Storm, *trump*, or the sad way COVID-19 was managed in the US, the lyric addresses the political fires of any season.

America to me I see you naked
But others see just what they want to see
Sweet America eulogize America then fall down on your knees and cry
I love California
But I'm watching it die
I'm watching it die!
Sweet America think about America then fall down on your knees and cry

I had picked another Barry song, '*Dorothy's Daughter*,' for the B Side. I loved the airy feel to the major seventh chords, and breezy lyric. *'Sure, I like it when young ladies come into my room, sure I like it when they share my hammock. But Dorothy's Daughter is the best for me.'* We duplicated the '*Sweet America*' process, but the result was not the same. Kevin and Lol could not quite understand the song, or my vision, or perhaps they did not care. We spent some time on it, but I eventually surrendered, and the result was a shoddy recording. To this day I see it as a missed opportunity. I was intimidated. Lesson learned.

The Beatles, and George Martin, taught us that focus on the 'B' side was important. *'This Boy,' 'Rain,' 'The Inner Light.'* You are as strong as your weakest link. You must put in as much time as the work requires. 10cc had put their hearts into '*Sweet America*', but then their energy was gone. *'It is only the 'B' side.'* In any area of life, to get the maximum return, one must exert maximum effort. Hindsight shows that we should have recorded the 'B' side as a simple guitar and voice recording as it was intended. 10cc historically had forgettable B sides on their singles, '*Hot Sun Rock*', '*4% of Something*', Channel Swimmer', and 'Bee in My Bonnet'.

The good news, we had two tracks, recorded and mixed.

Harvey Lisberg made an immediate deal with Philips Records, and '*Sweet America*' was soon released in Europe. Lisberg was a powerful man in the industry and seemed to get whatever he wanted from the record label. The air was thick with anticipation. To celebrate the signing with this Dutch Record Label, me and the four members of 10cc went to the premiere of the theatrical release of '*Woodstock: The Movie*', at the Odeon in Deansgate. They arrived in four separate cars. Three identical Lotus's, and one Aston Martin, with me in the passenger seat. A night to remember. The highlight of the film was the Santana set, unbelievable.

The radio acceptance of '*Sweet America*' was instant. It was named Tony Blackburn's BBC Record of the Week. The week preceding it was '*Another Day*' by Paul McCartney, his first single outside The Beatles. The week following was '*Ticket to Ride*' by the Carpenters. Solid bookends.

At 7:45am, that Monday to that Friday, Tony announced the *BBC Record of the week*. I listened on my transistor radio all five days as trumpets blared to announce that the next four minutes belonged to England's BBC 1's pick of that week, *'Barry Greenfield's Sweet America.'* I was over the moon. The BBC played it a great deal throughout the day and evening. Each time announcing its status as Record of the Week. This was the BBC. The British Broadcasting Corporation. The channel that Englishmen, listened to as Winston Churchill gave speeches throughout the horrific Second World War.

The song got attention certainly, but I think its subject matter, America, did not quite connect with the English listener. One can never ascertain why some art works commercially, and another piece does not. It faded from the radio after a month.

I was mildly disappointed, but I had already decided that I would not continue with the Strawberry team. I needed more time to mature, to prepare and learn more about recording. I was still in middle school. I flew home to Vancouver with a lot to think about. Lisberg was not pleased.

Two years later I signed with LA's RCA records, I had had two more years of work under my belt. A boatload of concerts, a number one record, *'New York is Closed Tonight'*, plus four of my songs recorded by other acts. I had matured. The decision to not continue with Kennedy Street proved wise.

When I flew to LA for two days of discussion with Don Berkheimer, VP RCA America in 1973, I explained that I needed input in how my songs sounded and were arranged. I was not seeking control, merely a seat at the table. He agreed, thinking that my sitting at the table was essential. That is the way Lou Adler saw it with Carole King, and Tommy West and Terry Cashman imagined it with Jim Croce. 10cc did not see it that way. Strawberry felt wrong. Everything felt rushed. No Zen. I sat quietly, ignored by Graham, who made the error that many producers do. He did not get the artists' input. The creator always has a vision, that should be explored. The best producers I have worked with, Chris Nole, in Nashville, David Kershenbaum, in LA, were in essence co-producers.

Another example of how to best produce a folk artist is found in studying the stellar work of Milt Okun. Okun who initially produced records for The Chad Mitchell Trio and folk group Peter, Paul and Mary, which still sound full many years later. Okun graduated to produce numerous hit songs, and many LPs, for the legendary songwriter, John Denver. Okun understood that keeping it softer matches the heart and soul of a folkies music. Two in tune duos, songwriter and producer, are Cat Stevens and Paul Samwell-Smith, '*The Wind*' and '*Peace Train*'. and Melanie and her husband Peter Schekeryk, who produced the song '*Brand New Key*' and others for this delightful folk artist. As with all things in life, you are only as strong as your weakest link.

Other songs that illustrates how *a good marriage* benefits the song, are '*Hey Jude*', by McCartney, a sad lament about divorce, and the children that suffer from it, is perfect, in mood and content. And '*Laléna*' by Donovan, produced expertly by Mickie Most who selected sweet strings to accent a hauntingly beautiful folk-flavored ballad which gets stronger with each listen. Gems both. The writer and the producer took the time to meld.

To explain this concept, I share a paragraph from *Donovan Unofficial* about the origin of 'Laléna' my favourite Donovan song. (1)

In 2004, Donovan revealed that the song was inspired by the actress Lotte Lenya and that the song's lyrics, addressed to a societally marginalized woman, were Donovan's reaction to Lenya's character in the film version of The Threepenny Opera:
   She's a streetwalker, but in the history of the world, in all nations, women have taken on various roles from priestess to whore to mother to maiden to wife. This guise of sexual power is very prominent, and therein I saw the plight of the character. Women have roles thrust upon them and make the best they can out of them, so I'm describing the character Lotte Lenya is playing, and a few other women I've seen during my life, but it's a composite character of women who are outcasts on the edge of society.
   Donovan sharing the thinking about his character with his producer, Mickie Most, would provide the recording with a roadmap. The melancholy of the opus was captured by the producer

who understood what the songwriter wanted to convey to his audience with this beautiful piece.

Wind the clock ahead twenty-two years, to 1992, and Graham and Eric, the remaining members of 10cc are in New York recording 10cc's, 'Meanwhile'.

Gouldman writes about the producer artist relationship on the 10cc website, *10cc.world: (2)*

After many years apart, pursuing different projects, Eric and I got back together to write a new batch of songs. All was going well until we started recording in New York. Our record company wanted us to have an American producer, Gary Katz. Unfortunately, this album suffered from a lack of communication between us and Gary. He seemed to spend more time on the phone than in the control room. Eric left the recording early. Bad vibes all round. Consequently, I cannot listen to 'Meanwhile.'

In this paragraph Gouldman agrees with my philosophy, harmony between producer and artist is an important ingredient in a studio recording. Gary Katz is the man who sat in the producer's chair with America's best band, Steely Dan. But according to Gouldman, Gary did not seem to care about him. Passion between the producer, the artist, the players, the engineer is paramount. Gary Katz in my books is one of the finest record producers of all time.

My recordings in Hollywood in 1973, 'Blue Sky', and in Nashville in 2008, 'Exposed Soul', had that magic. All the pieces working in harmony, at full tilt, anchors aweigh, the proof is in the pudding.

    I had lived in the Gouldman's Crumpsall two-bedroom flat. A blissful period in my life. Fun and songwriting school. I wrote the lyrics, and he wrote the melodies. The master and the apprentice. I was living a dream. A lovely home, no rent to find, kindness at every turn, and musical growth. I am godfather to Sarah their first born. Most days we would drive to his parent's townhome, 20 minutes away. We would take our guitars. My cheap one, his, a beautiful Gibson Everly, and slip into the small bedroom where he was raised. The same room where the 'hits' were created. *'Bus*

Stop', '*Heart Full of Soul.*' I learned lessons collaborating with a master. Discipline. Write everything down, whether you use it or not. Take breaks. Graham worked 11am to 5pm, with an hour for lunch. A white bread sandwich and soup. Betty made the lunch and ate with us. Hymie and Betty Gouldman called me their second son. I adored them both.

Five decades later Graham now 78, and I are still in contact. I stay connected with Lisberg, who at 84 is retired and living in Palm Springs. One thing I have learnt in my seven decades of walking this earth, people are who they are, if someone shows you who they are, believe them.

Every brick in my wall is an important brick. 1971, in '*Strawberry North*', taught me how to work with others. It is essential to be courageous and to offer your input. In 1971 I did not. In 1973, and onwards, I did. If one does not learn from one's mistakes, history will repeat.

1. '*Laléna*'   *Donovan   Unofficial.   Retrieved 2 October 2016.*
2. *Graham Gouldman 10cc world.*

6

My first tour
On the road with John Lee Hooker 1972

My personal musical choices were born out of the music my family listened to at home on our hi-fi. Frank Sinatra, Petula Clark, Frankie Vaughan, 'The Velvet Fog' Mel Tormé, Alma Cogan, and my favourite voice, Perry Como. Plus, my father sang their songs as a crooner with a Manchester big band, his stage name was Bernard Grey. We were never offered the Blues, or Jazz to inspect at home. We were never blessed with ethnic music, or the beauty of classical symphonies.

When Elvis arrived in the mid-fifties he was never invited to perform in our house. Our staple diet was 100% Wonder Bread. I was raised on a steady diet of mainstream, white, considered good looking, usually smiling, singers. Nat King Cole and The Mills Brothers were the only exceptions.

In 1963 'Please Please Me', arrived, and my musical choices continued in that vein, music made by white musicians. The first LP I purchased was 'Beatles for Sale,' followed by 'In Touch with Peter and Gordon'. I chose white radio music. The Kinks, The Hollies, The Rolling Stones, The Beatles, Donovan, Adam Faith, The Dave Clark Five. However, Cliff Richard and Anthony Newley was not on my list, I preferred living at the edge of town.

I knew a little about Motown music. Little Steve Wonder, The Shirelles, Smokey Robinson, and The Temptations. I had a deep respect for 'My Cherie Amour', 'Will You Still Love Me Tomorrow', 'Tears of a Clown', and 'My Girl', and most certainly, 'Reach Out I'll Be Tere' by The Four Tops. But I never used my hard-earned pocket money to bring that vinyl home.

I read the British music magazines. Rave, NME, and Melody Maker. Posters of Ray Davies, John Lennon, Bob Dylan and Keith

Richards, adorned my bedroom walls. Scotch tape hidden under each corner, posters rotated frequently.

The Blues' section in my local record store, had zero pull for me. I thought it to be boring 12 Bar stuff. It all sounded identical to my untrained ears. I had never heard the names John Lee Hooker, Muddy Waters, Ethel Waters or Robert Johnson. My life was simple, 'You Really Got Me,' 'Glad All Over', 'I'm Alive', 'Downtown,' and 'Walk on By'.

This all changed with a phone call on a Sunday in the dog days of summer 1972. 'New York is Closed Tonight,' sat atop the charts and with it the doors and windows were flung wide-open. Here comes the sun in the form of a mid afternoon telephone call from Hank Zevallos, the owner of Earth Breeze Productions. Hank was from LA, an American who like many, was having great difficulty with the US draft. Hank's right-hand man was James Conrad, a West Coast Tour promoter. They were clever, they had vision and tons of courage, and they were able to dream. We matched up perfectly. Hank's company, Earth Breeze Productions, offered me thirteen Canadian concert dates to co-headline with John Lee Hooker.

'Who is that?'

I asked naively, regretting the question the second I spoke the words. In today's world with Google, ignorance is easily rectified, back then we were somewhat lost.

Hank laughed. He explained the important role that Hooker had played in musical history. A highly thought of American Blues artist.

Hank said John Lee was 65, but later John Lee explained to me 'I dunno when I was born, maybe 1912, maybe 1917'. His age remains unknown. For Hank, the most important aspect of this pairing was that John and Barry would sell tickets to two different audiences. I loved the concept. I was thrilled to be considered. I accepted the tour. A dream offer, and a new challenge for me to relish. The tour would start on 17 August 1972 and end on 2 September 1972.

The itinerary was fabulous. Edmonton Jubilee; Lethbridge Civic; Trail Cominco Arena; Prince George Duchess Park Auditorium; Kamloops Memorial Arena; Penticton Peach Bowl; Nanaimo Civic Arena; Vancouver, Queen Elizabeth Theatre;

Calgary Jubilee; Saskatoon Centennial; Fort Williams Gardens; Winnipeg Centennial; and finally, Regina Center of the Arts. Thirteen brilliant stops. I get to travel Canada. I get paid, $400 a night, plus per diem, plus lodgings and transport. And most important I get to share my music for the first time in arenas and plush soft seat theatres. A dream come true. Can I pull this off?

Hank and James became my travel companions on this road adventure. Especially James, with whom I am still in contact with to this day. James and I have compared notes, memories, and photographs taken, plus journal details that helped in the research of this chapter. We both really liked John, and he remembers how close John and I became. John needed a young man's help to get through the hotels, airports etc. and I needed a mentor to learn about playing live.

Sound checks would be a new experience. Travel with musicians would be a new experience. A different bed in a new hotel every night. Plus, these guys were serious experienced players. Been there, done that. Their cups were filled to the brim with decades of live work. I had struck gold. I was about to perform in front of thousands. Fresh eyes, and fresh ears, every night. I was the virgin; John Lee Hooker was the salty dog.

I had played lots of small venues, successfully. After much trial and error, I had developed an hour set, eleven songs. My set list had thirty plus original songs to choose from. I knew what the first three would be, then I would pick the remaining songs from what was on my list, based on my audiences energetic feedback. It worked will. The largest audience had been four hundred. Usually, one hundred plus in a club setting. My intention was to stay close to the set list, and format, I had developed. Why fix what was not broken. I enjoyed every performance in my short career to date.

Who was John Lee Hooker?

I know now, what I did not know then, that John Lee Hooker was an American legend, a great songwriter. 'Boom Boom' is a song written by John and recorded 26 October 1961. It became a Blues standard. He was a unique, if not always, brilliant guitarist. The son of a sharecropper. John shared great stories with me, in wonderful detail, in the weeks to come. His history was colourful, Black American History. At times painful, but always fascinating.

John loved to share with me. I loved to dig deep into his past. I listened attentively and with a genuine heart.

Hooker rose to prominence performing an electric guitar-style adaptation of Delta Blues, that he developed in Detroit. He often incorporated other elements, including Talking Blues and early North Mississippi Hill Country Blues. He developed his own driving-rhythm boogie style, distinct from the 1930s–1940s piano-derived boogie-woogie.

This was my first opportunity at the real deal. I was not sure where to start. I asked how long I needed my set to be? 45 minutes. Anchors aweigh! Eighteen days on the road. A small suitcase, three blue denim work shirts, an extra pair of clean blue-jeans, five tee-shirts, a jumper for the cold, my big jacket, a baseball cap for the rain, an extra pair of shoes, my Gurian and Ovation guitars, strings, plectrums and a smile in my pocket. I hopped into a taxi for the ride downtown, and then I jumped onto the tour bus with John. Away we go. Edmonton here we come. It would be an all day and into the night drive.

The tour's opening night was at the Jubilee Theatre in Edmonton, and it was an amazing experience. A lush, plush, 2800 soft seater. Great sound. Great sight lines. Great night. I was well received. I made them laugh. I sounded crystal clear, and I was 'present'. I earned an encore, and the audience stood up to clap, after 'New York is Closed Tonight.' They sang along at the tag of that song, as I do to this very day. The sing along to the la la la part may have started that night; I cannot be certain.

'I had done good!'

The promoters were pleased. Tickets sold well, and John and I were slowly becoming connected. We were together a great deal for the next eighteen days. I became his bud. He mine. Polite, loquacious at times. Moody and quiet too. Angry at things. He easily fell into an aggressive manner with others. He ranted at his band, railed at servers at Denny's, and he was always angry with his son, who was his band leader.

To me, John seemed old (young people thought anyone over fifty was old, over sixty-five ancient), Black (like Mississippi), really cool (Miles Davis cool), and uber talented (Keith Richards talented).

The first hotel, in Edmonton, set the tone for the tour. It was not as nice as the Holiday Inn, closer to Motel 6, but a notch above. I cannot remember the name. John insisted that he and I were on the same floor, at this and every stop on the tour. Fine with me. I was there to learn from a master, who loved to teach. I was the grasshopper, he the sensei.

The next gig, in Lethbridge, Alberta, was equally amazing. The Civic Hockey rink. Sold out. Noisy kids. The rink stunk of beer, and it reeked of pot. It was 1972. A Rock and Blues crowd. Male dominated, but some females who were more in tune with my art it seemed. I played mainly songs from my 'Blue Sky' LP, it was received better than I could have guessed. They all knew 'New York is Closed Tonight.' Again, they laughed at my humour.

The promoter was thrilled. We all were. I was growing in confidence. If I forgot a lyric I would improvise. If I messed up a melody, nobody knew but me. I made sure to smile and not rush. Those are two things John taught me that I think about to this day. I waited eagerly throughout the day, for each set that began at 8pm. I had found a heavenly place for almost an hour.

I did 50 minutes of original Barry music, plus encore. I told stories about each song. I did a nine-song set, 'Jack and Jill' 'Sweet America', 'How Long', then an encore or two. We took an intermission. It was followed by John's band minus John, and they would entertain. Playing 20 minutes of standard 12-Bar instrumentals. They were, and I am being kind, average. Then John walked out. He sat on a hard chair centre-stage. He hit his electric hard and true. He demanded attention and he got it. John's set was received wildly. The boys in the crowd came to taste the real Blues, and John Lee Hooker delivered. He took no prisoners.

His four-piece Band, called the Coast-to-Coast Blues Band, was led by his unruly son John Jr. John Lee threw him off the road mid-tour. Uncomfortable for all. Hard drugs were the son's vice. I witnessed the procurement, and the affect. Not pretty. Scary for me, and unsettling for John, a father. It was a world I had never seen, never known.

I did radio interviews in each stop, to sell seats. The DJ's asked questions that were standard, but I enjoyed the attention, and the chance to practice my spiel. My song was at number one in the charts. I tasted fame with a small 'f.'

'How long you been doing this?;' 'Do you write your own material?'; 'What music do you play at home?'

Each night I watched John's set top-to-tale. Usually from the wings but occasionally I put on a baseball cap, and I headed into the room. That way I got a different ambience, and better sound. Sometimes an audience member would recognize me and speak kindly and complimentary. I got a few smiles from the ladies, and that was nice.

After each show we would return to John's hotel room, so that I could count his gig-pay for him. He insisted on being paid in cash, and he liked me to check that it was accurate. It was. John told me stories of how, over the years, he had been swindled, many times, by unscrupulous promoters. Rascals, thieves, who disappeared mid-show with the door money. Leaving the artists with no renumeration.

A year later I played a show with the Pointer Sisters. It was at the Vancouver Orpheum. The Pointer Sisters were booked to begin their set at 9.15pm, 15 minutes after I had completed my set. They refused to go onstage without being paid in advance, in cash. Their set eventually began at 10.35pm. The promoter had to get the cash from the box office. It was very uncomfortable for all involved. I felt that the paying audience were being shortchanged by all parties. I recall it was a tense uncomfortable-night for me, despite the fact that I had earned an Orpheum two-encore set.

The Hooker style of guitar playing has been imitated but never matched. As opposed to the 12-bar blues that became a form of mainstream, post-war party music, Hooker's Blues is often based on just one chord pulled to its limits. With his right hand and foot, he keeps the rhythm: the thumping bedrock for his lyrics, which he delivers in an emphatic speak-sing, shaped by a childhood spent listening to church sermons and local Blues singers. He became a musical hero to me.

John Lee and I ate dinner together. Each meal we had, was at a local, ordinary street café. Sandwich and fries for John. Soup and a burger for me. We both varied our selection at times, but usually that. John refused to try Chinese or non-American cuisine. I capitulated. I would rather eat with John than not eat with John.

In that greasy-spoon booth we really talked. Food is social, and people talk openly, honestly and intimately when eating. He would pull out his pipe after eating, and we would sit and chat till he grew tired. It was delightful. He covered his long past in some detail. I listened to his story of the South, and a shared my life living in an apartheid world. John asked about my introduction to African music with African street players. He was fascinated by my story which was a great compliment to my 21-year-old ears. I had some of my best times ever, over those thirteen live nights.

One special night was in Thunder Bay, Ontario.

Most days we rode the tour bus with the other players. But Thunder Bay was too far to spend in the bus from Saskatoon for John and Barry. The tour was a success, profits were being made by the promoters, and we were rewarded. The two headliners were treated to a private Cessna. All others were on the long-haul bus ride. John, me, and the pilot. We were a bit freaked; the pilot was smoking weed, all flight! But we survived.

We talked all day. It was on that day that John told me he invented the word 'boogie.'

John Lee Hooker had his first hit single with "Boogie Chillum" in 1948. Producer Bernard Basman recorded him alone at the microphone with an electric guitar. A second microphone was placed in a wooden pallet beneath his feet to capture the sound of his foot stomping to the rhythm. Now that's music! In his deep, growl-like stammering voice. John's roots mesmerized me. So real.

'Yeh Barry I am the fool who invented the word boogie.' I done it for my song Boogie Chillun.'

> Boogie Chillun
> One night I was layin' down
> I heard mama 'n papa talkin'
> I heard papa tell mama
> "Let that boy boogie-woogie
> It's in him, and it got to come out"
> And I felt so good
> And I went on boogie'n just the same.

That lyric, his voice, his originality, his truth, sums up his act.

The day of the Thunder Bay concert we were showcased to the town in a parade, in a bunch of vintage cars through the city streets. It was ridiculous.

Me, Kent Collenger, and James Conrad, crammed into a single vintage car. John and his band in a few others. Honking the horns, as we drove the main streets. Thunder Bay had folks waiving back at us. It really helped sell the show, and we had an audience of 12,000 in the arena that night. The promoter got the mega-bucks, John and I got our regular fee.

Thunder Bay was the big one. The Fort Williams Gardens Arena sold out. A big barn where Thunder Bay hockey ruled. I loved that night. Wild. Exciting. Brash. I really let go. John was John and they loved him. Every show I was transfixed by his voice, his Gibson at Spinal Tap eleven, and his presence. He had the power of Stevie Ray Vaughan, the charisma of Buddy Guy, and the understanding of Santana.

All the 'stars' I have met have changed my music. They all had a lesson for me. Graham Gouldman was 'work hard.' Rodger Hodgson was 'courage,' Mel Torme showed me that they are not all nice. The Fifth Dimension taught 'kindness and humility.' John Lee Hooker, like Kenny Rogers a few years earlier, taught me to play only because you 'love to play,' and always sing like an 'original.' John was all street. A true Southern man.

He and I grew close, and I felt like he lived and breathed musical history. John was extremely supportive of my music. Flattering at times. I played John songs that I had written in the hotels . One was 'Concert Fever'. We had two sleeps in Thunder Bay. So, I wrote for hours. 'Concert Fever' was about that tour. John loved it and sang the chorus a lot.

> A young miner in the Black Hills
> Is digging for some gold
> And thinking about his lady
> He harvested back home
> And like a boxer in a fight
> Who's humming in the ring
> His melody like mine
> Is the song his lady sings
> It grows cold as I drive into each town

> And oh that concert fever
> It turns me upside down
> And the only way
> To pass the time of day
> Is to sing the song you sang
> To fill the time that I'm away
> And oh that concert fever

I paid homage to Neil Young with, 'He harvested back home', and Paul Simon with the couplet, 'And like a boxer in a fight, who's humming in the ring'. Two of my favourite writers.

I learnt how to chat between songs on that tour. It is an important component for a singer songwriter. John spoke little on stage. But his voice was so bass strong, so Southern in timbre, and he demanded the audience's attention with each simple guitar flourish, or vocal nuance.

We made a great team for the show. Barry Greenfield singing personal heart centred songs, about love, politics, and life. John Lee Hooker banging out electric Southern Blues, 'First Time I Met The Blues' and 'Talk To Me Baby (I Can't Hold Out)'.

Each show was well received. Each show was a challenge, and I grew as a performer. Playing consecutive nights is a real help in the improvement of the show. How to tightens parts. What to keep in. What to drop out.

The tour went fast, and by the final date we had a great rhythm and camaraderie.

I cannot recall the last day or night in Regina, with much detail, but I was sad that it was over. We flew back to Vancouver together; I would miss my friend.

John and I never crossed paths again after that tour. He passed in 2001. I learnt that I loved playing live. I loved the road. I loved John Lee Hooker.

Seems like yesterday, but it was 50 years ago. I was new to the music business. What a fine teacher John Lee Hooker was to me. Thank you, Sir!

Footnote:

Opposites attract. A 65-year-old Mississippi Blues legend meets a 21-year-old Mancunian folk singer, and they gel. They relate. They care about each other.

Although we appeared on the same bill, I never played guitar, wrote with, or sang a note with John Lee Hooker, but it was music that we had in common. Yes, we loved music. But we loved life identically.

I smiled through all three weeks with John. I learnt how to play live on this tour. John Lee Hooker was true to himself; I have tried to emulate that. In my song writing, my parenting, my being a husband, and a friend, and in every page, and with every tale, in this book.

Keep it honest and accurate as best you are able.

7

The recording of Blue Sky in RCA Hollywood 1973

Back in the halcyon days of the early seventies my life focus became clearer. My journey into music grew more comfortable. More natural. The transitions when changing guitar chords improved too, became smoother. I managed to tune my guitar more easily. I could sense a maturity in my song's subject matter. I worked harder. Longer hours. I became more dedicated to my craft. Studying the methods of the best. Standing on the shoulder of giants. Art for arts sake.

Playing live each weekend in music rooms that held a hundred, or more, proved to be fallow ground for my art to grow. Singing and playing in the light. These forty-five-minute showcases proved to be the perfect classroom to learn and improve. I was twenty-two, and I could sense I was developing a small following. I made repeated stops at the Egress, the Roller Rink, and at Rohan's. I began tasting Canada. Edmonton had the Side Track Cafe, Calgary, U of C, in Toronto I played at a Blues Bar on Queens Street. I did two nights in Halifax. That one was not a success. Poor sound, no interest from the small crowd. My most upsetting night was at The Ting in Winnipeg. My guitar was broken by a drunk who pushed the speaker over, onto it. I had a back up guitar, always do, but the owner of the room refused to compensate my loss. I quickly learnt, and accepted, that some nights were diamonds, and some nights were stones.

I opened for Steve Martin, John Hartford, Cheech and Chong, and Mose Allison, among others. I shared headline status with C.B. Victoria, Chilliwack and Sandalspring. I no longer wanted to be a lawyer, a teacher, or a university professor. I wanted to be a singer-songwriter. The one fact that I am certain about, is that in all these countless early gigs, the highlight one was co-headlining with John

Lee Hooker. Thirteen dates, coast to coast. That series of concerts benefitted my art significantly.

As 1972 drew to a close I had already taken two important steps in this odyssey.

Step one, 1968, I received the positive approval from Apple Records and John Lennon. Apple arrived too early, I was unprepared, and not ready to wear that mantle.

Step two, 1970, found me in Manchester England with Harvey Lisberg and 10cc. I felt too little synchronicity with that meld.

These two steps were my dress rehearsal for the arrival of step three, 1973, RCA, and the songs I had written for *'Blue Sky'*. Here I sensed was the yellow brick road.

In Lyman Frank Baum's, *'Wizard of Oz'*, the yellow brick road is a metaphor for the belief that streets are paved with gold. Another interpretation is that the yellow brick road symbolizes what's known in Buddhism and Kabbalah as The Golden Path. It was exciting to walk through a door having no idea what awaited me in the room I was about to enter, the big time. I was headed to The City of Angels. How did I get this opportunity to record my songs in Hollywood?

My day-to-day life was repetitive and simple, I was plugging away at my Arts degree, majoring in English Literature, at the University of British Columbia, the intention was to enter law school. The daily menu read, bus to school, go to my job, and when the weekend arrived play a set or two. A full plate.

It was a Friday evening, and I was at my weekend job at The Bay department store, selling teen clothing, two dollars an hour, working to enable me to pay for my rent and food. I decided, bravely, to approach the stores General Manager, to suggest that I could, should, write a jingle for the store's teen department. It could be used on local radio. He laughed. I am sure he was thinking *'why not, the kids an employee?'* and he agreed to listen to my submission. I went home and I wrote a sixty second jingle for the store, to use to promote *'Vibrations'*, the teen clothing department on the second floor, where I worked twenty hours a week. Saturday morning before the store opened, I went to the ostentatious GM office at The Bay, and I played my submission. He loved it and ordered a cheque for $600 for the production budget. '*It worked*!'

I booked some time at Tom Northcott's Studio 3 on twelfth avenue in Vancouver and the *Vibrations* jingle took me an hour to record. That meant; after paying the studio fees for the production, I had $450 remaining to spend on other music. I decided to record a new song, '*New York is Closed Tonight*', my song about pollution in the Big Apple. I used two players that were in he studio that afternoon, $25 each. I played the rest. Sang, and hit a drum with a stick.

Then a miracle happened. My guardian angel popped up again. Bo Diddley was performing in Vancouver that weekend. My bassist, a concert journalist and reviewer for the Province newspaper, Ken Lundgren, played a cassette copy of the track to the legend in his dressing room during a post-show interview. Yes, Bo Diddley heard '*New York is Closed Tonight.*' He asked if he could take the cassette of the song to Fred Ahlert Jr. in Manhattan, the Music Publisher of Bacharach and David. A business connection of Bo's. Ken eagerly agreed. Sometimes truth is stranger than fiction.

A week later Fred called me at my home. Interestingly in 1972, the singer songwriter had yet to be invented. The call came before the success of Carole King, James Taylor and Cat Stevens. His potent New York accent came through clearly.

'Barry, your song New York is Closed Tonight' is a #1 song, and I want to get you a deal!'

Flattered yes, but after the 10cc adventure, I was not ready, or willing to jump back into the fire.

'No thanks. I am going to complete my Batchelor of Arts, and then apply for Law School.'

I have always been, and remain, a blend of conservative and rebel. A law degree felt wise.

For 6 months Fred would call from time to time. My answer never varied. Flattered yes, but motivated no. Then one day he invited me to join him in San Francisco for lunch. I told him that I could not afford to fly anywhere. He said,

'Go to Vancouver Airport, Air Canada, and a return-ticket will be waiting for you. I'll have a limousine pick you up at San

Francisco Airport.' I weighed the pros and cons. I acquiesced and said,
   'Alright Fred, I look forward to meeting you tomorrow afternoon'.

Over halibut, broccoli and rice in a Fisherman's Wharf sea food restaurant, Fred promised me dreams of grandeur. His flattery, positivity, and persuasive logic, worked. I signed the contract he brought to the meeting. I flew home happy.

Fred Ahlert Jr. was rich, famous and powerful. He really believed that my song about New York was a hit song, and he explained to me how hard it is to write a hit song, and how difficult that is for him to find the perfect beast.

Fred Ahlert Jr. inherited his Fathers Publishing Empire. His father Fred Ahlert Sr. opened his successful Publishing company in 1928. Fred Sr. was inducted into the Songwriters Hall of Fame in 1970. Their catalogue included Ella Fitzgerald, Louis Armstrong, and Nat King Cole. Fred Jr. had inherited this million-dollar catalogue. To add more bricks into the wall, Fred Jr. published Bacharach and David, the US equivalent to Lennon and McCartney. *'Walk On By', 'Raindrops keep Falling On My Head', 'Close To You'.* Fred was the destination I had been looking for since my dream of being a songwriter was born. That is how things operated back then. John and Paul signed such a deal with Dick James, Northern Songs Ltd in 1963. He was their Fred Ahlert Jr. The Bee Gees had Robert Stigwood in their corner. Bob Dylan signed with New Yorks manager Albert Grossman, after months of courting. Then the train started moving pretty quickly for Bob. Peter, Paul and Mary scored a huge hit with his early gem, *'Blowin' In The Wind'.* It is always a suit that makes the difference for the artist. Some suits are decent folk, some suits are not.

Fred worked fast and delivered all he had promised me at that luncheon. Within a few weeks he secured a Canadian release, on Laurie Records, NY, and soon *'New York is Closed Tonight'* was on the radio, often. Fred was a powerful, alpha male, and he knew how to manoeuvre in the music business of the day. Three months later *'New York is Closed Tonight'* was #1 on the Canadian Charts and stayed there for weeks. It won the '1972 *Harold Moon Socan award for excellence in Canadian Music'.* Fred prediction on that first phone call was accurate. *'Barry, your song 'New York is Closed Tonight' is a #1 song!'.*

Without any further input, or discussion with me the artist, Fred parlayed that success into a deal with RCA America. Fred got a $20,000 US advance, and an offer to record an LP of my original material. Early 1973, I was flying south chasing the sun, to the City of Angels.

I am unaware as to how the RCA arrangement played out, or if there were any other interested parties. Fred saw my input as being irrelevant. He had my signature, allowing him, as my manager, carte-blanche to sign on my behalf. I just accepted and trusted. As Schultz would mutter in Hogan's Heroes. *'I know nothing!'*

A chauffeured, shiny, black limousine was waiting curbside for me at LAX. The driver, patiently standing inside the terminal held a sign that read 'Barry Greenfield'. I was floating downstream, in comfortable Corinthian leather, destination the Hollywood Holiday Inn. Fred secured a deal. I was treated with kid-gloves by RCA. Chauffeured here and there; and they wanted me to pick the LP's producer. RCA selected three producers for me to meet, and interview.

A Producer is one of the key elements in the recording process. That role can add or subtract. I learnt that lesson in Stockport in 1970 with 10cc. The fact that RCA were allowing me to interview, and select, candidates, is an indication how RCA worked. They understood that if they were going to invest a great deal of capital into the act, then they should trust the act. I believe that this thinking by the Corporation is one of the reasons that I flourished at RCA.

The first candidate that I met in a large RCA office, alone, was Paul Rothchild, The Doors producer; second, another equally famous older man whose name I cannot recall, and lastly the staff producer, an unknown, 25 years old, David M. Kershenbaum. I spent ten minutes with the first two, and forty-five with David. No contest, I picked David Kershenbaum. The other two guys were there for the cheque.

The rookie, a young David Kershenbaum would have a long career. David went on to produce seventy-five international gold and platinum albums, win multiple Grammys and he would receive a prestigious Oscar nomination for Michael Kamen and Bryan Adams song *'Everything I do I do it for You'*. Later in his illustrious career Kershenbaum became an executive at three major record companies. It all started for him with *'Blue Sky'*, his first job in the producer's chair.

The next morning, I was at the home of the music arranger Jimmie Haskell, top of the class. Jimmie had won an Oscar and Grammies. Plus, his work history is staggering, *'Ode to Billie Joe'*, 'If you Leave Me Now', and the classic *'Bridge over Troubled Water'*, amongst others. A hero to me.

Jimmie and Mrs. Haskell welcomed me like an old friend. Tea, chat and hard work were on the agenda. Their home was warm and cozy, and opulent. We worked for three long, wonderful days. Me playing my gurian acoustic, and he on Fender Rhodes. When done, we had all the sheet music ready for the Studio. Twelve Barry songs! Guitar, piano, percussion, vocal arrangements, all planned and charted by the best arranger in the US. A solid foundation to build on.

'Jack and Jill', *'Concert Fever'*, *'Sweet America'* and the rest. Jimmie asked me to share my reason and thought behind each composition. The mood that I was thinking. He had used his gifts with all the heroes in my back pocket. An unending list of the most popular artists, including Elvis, Neil Diamond, CSN, Steely Dan, Billy Joel and my all-time number one American combo Simon and Garfunkel. In my five decades I have never worked with anyone whom I respect more than Haskell. He was diligent, brilliant, and full of love. The three days flew past like the Shinkansen, a Japanese bullet train.

I needed a break to think and rest. RCA gave me one day off. I ate lunch at Arby's (a US Fast-food chain, known for its roast beef, fries and shakes on Sunset Boulevard). I became aware of correct food choices when my daughter was born. Then a lazy afternoon swimming in the hotel pool, finally I walked for hours down Sunset Boulevard, absorbing the culture. I crawled into bed at nine. Me was my only company all day.

I was living on the 5th Floor of The Holiday Inn. A standard 4-star room. I saw interesting musicians in the elevator. I cannot recall names, but I did get silently starstruck at least twice. The Holiday Inn was the centre of the universe for visiting musicians of the day.

One highlight was having breakfast most mornings at the Inn, at eight am. I shared coffee, toast and marmalade with Slade and David Foster. We chatted about music, life, The Beatles, and the business. Slade were lovely, average working-class Brits from Wolverhampton. They were voted the most successful British group of the seventies. Foster was in
    LA recording an album with his band, Attitude. A year later he invited me to
    co-write and record a song to raise funds for Oxfam. I sang the lyrics I had written for the project; he arranged and produced the session. It was a wonderful experience, and it was my initial foray in using my art to raise funds for charitable causes. I continue that practice to this day. I appreciated the invite.

I awoke each morning, with the rooster, at the crack of dawn. I worked on the song that I would be recording that day. At half-nine, the RCA transport was in front of the Inn waiting for me. An all-access laminate on a lanyard around my neck. The quiet Larry Knechtel (Bread bass player and pianist, and the man who played the piano on *'Bridge Over Troubled Water'*) was the first to arrive. We sat on the control room couch drinking strong, black, coffee, from our RCA mugs. Then Larry Carlton popped in with a warm hello. Larry, who was then, and still is, a giant in the industry, had his small caravan filled with his acoustic guitars, mandolins, Stratocasters, Gibson's et. al. accompanied with a guitar technician who would assist him throughout the day. I hired two drummers. Jim Gordon (Derek and the Dominoes) for the power tunes, and Russel Kunkel (Carole King) for the heart centred songs. Finally, Joe Osborn (The Wrecking Crew, Simon, and Garfunkel) and his custom Fender bass. The business end of the team, Haskell, Kershenbaum and the sound engineers, Peter Abbott, and Rick Ruggieri, (Elvis, Neil Diamond), were already in place doing their thing. Microphone placement, amps set, all directed by Kershenbaum and Ruggieri, and was completed before I arrived. Adjustments, and fine tuning to the set up, completed before the red light went on.

The day began at ten sharp, with the Boys forming a circle in the room, me at the centre. I sat on a chair and played the song-of-the-day for them, as it was written, and incorporating the Haskell tweaks. I shared my thoughts about the songs feel, its opening, its closing, and the transitions. I was allowed to choose piano-based approach, or guitar-based approach. Input that I shared was the result of working with Haskell. All players were picked by Kershenbaum. Each was given a chart written by Haskell and me.

Questions flew at me. *'do you want this, Barry?'* *'will this idea work, Barry?'*

'I agree Barry, let's see if a mandolin will work' *'Brushes or sticks?'* *'Let's add a half bar here!'*

It blew my young mind to have my simple four-minute songs come alive in the hands, and through the hearts, of these amazing musicians. Carlton, Osborn, Gordon, Muhoberac, Kunkel and Knechtel. They were collectively known as double-scale musicians. That indicated that their fee was double union scale. RCA allowed me this very luxury which I assumed was not afforded to many. I think the appropriate phrase may be *'you get what you pay for.'* Professionalism at work, or in life, is natural to some, but not all. I have worked with less than perfect session players over the decades. Chalk and cheese.

I recall the rush we all felt when we had finished. Larry Carlton's guitar was so fine. Jim Gordon hit the drums with anger and great power. Guest pianist Larry Muhoberac (Sinatra) was used on *'Concert Fever'* and *'New York is Closed Tonight'* to great effect. Additional troops dropped by in the form of back up singers (Daniel J. Moore, Brooks Hunnicutt) and percussion (Gene Estes, Milt Holland).

Early evening, the Band were excused, and I entered the isolation booth to lay down vocals on the track recorded that day. This took a few hours. Doubling, harmonizing and all the recording was pure, no autotune etc. as is common today. This is why 1970's music, (Elton, King Crimson, Wings, Bowie, Joni Mitchell), feels and sounds superior to today's offerings. Kate Perry, Maroon 5, Bieber, Lady Gaga, Adele, Madonna, are perfect because they are manipulated by artificial intelligence, and they incorporate computers to remove every blemish and flaw. That is the music business today. The Eagles sing live, sometimes lip sync, they are assisted by pre-recorded tape and autotune. An older man can not reach the F# needed in the song that he sang at age 26.

I am a songwriter with a limited vocal range. But I had sung each *Blue-Sky* song a great many times in their creation. That provided me with a comfortable blueprint for the vocal delivery. However, Haskell had thrown in many nuances in the arrangement that improved the song. Kershenbaum also put his finger in the pie. It took me time to learn how to navigate these new twists and turns. David had acres of patience. Each day I grew and became stronger. It was fun. We did a song a day, some took two days. One of the most enjoyable days in Studio 'B' was recording a song I composed about my mother, *'Free the Lady.'* It was day three. The guys really connected to this song. I shared that it was written for my mother, and they all had mothers. We played it through using Haskell's arrangement and I got the idea to have an extended solo towards the tag. I realized that this came out of the blue, but Kershenbaum never said no to my ideas. In his long career I think he continued that approach. Joe Jackson, Tracey Chapman, Dylan, Cat Stevens to name but a few. Larry Muhobrac, (Muhoberac was the original keyboardist in Elvis Presley's TCB Band, Barbra Streisand, Seals and Crofts, and Neil Diamond) sat at the electric piano with eyes wide shut. In one take, we all created what lives on the LP track today. A long solo that flowed like the Mississippi. Don Berkheimer, Vice President of RCA, who later became the president, dropped in early on that session.

'I'm only popping by to say hello. Just a few minutes.'

He loved *'Free the Lady'* so much that he stayed three hours. Buying all the gang pizza. Nice guy Don. I did not partake in the meal; it affects the voice eating within two hours of vocalizing.

Another outstanding memory for me was the tracking of *'Concert Fever'*. The entire band stood at the end of the take and applauded.

My all-time favourite fifteen minutes, and the third outstanding memory of the three weeks in 'B', was the session where Larry Carlton played his extended guitar solo, at the end of *'New York is Closed Tonight'*. I sat down with Larry explaining how I was going to mimic McCartney's scream from Helter Skelter as best I could at the point where the song goes to the F dominant 9th chord before the songs long tag. I wanted him to capture that emotion on his Les Paul. I hoped my channelling Paul's moment would make sense to Larry. It did. He nailed it, and it is my favourite minute on *'Blue Sky'*. We were all beaming in the control room at the King of American guitar solos, Larry Carlton in full flight. Osborne, Gordon, Kershenbaum, Muhoberac and me.

Many years later Larry became a staple on the lead guitar for, in my opinion, America's greatest ever Band, Steely Dan. There are many examples of him reaching that height. *'Kid Charlemagne'* is certainly one.

Larry Carlton's multi-sectioned, cosmic-jazz lead in this cut may be the best of all: It is so complex it is a song in its own right. The lead lines by Larry in Dan's *'Kid Charlemagne'* are intense, fluid, and frequently on the brink of spinning out of control. Nick Hornby in Songbook, spoke of the solo's. *'extraordinary and dexterous exuberance.'* I describe his work on my track, *'New York is Closed Tonight,'* as personal, with the grace of an eagle flying above his prey planning a swoop. Thank you, Larry.

All the players on *'Blue Sky'* showed warmth and joy and seemed grateful to be together playing, and shaping, Barry songs. The bed we lay on was made by Jimmie Haskell. The room was lit by David Kershenbaum. I was blessed, and extremely fortunate, to have found Oz.

We worked solidly 5 days a week for three weeks. Recording the tracks, overdubs, and vocals. Mixing was done by Peter Abbot and Rick Ruggieri.

Mastering at the Mastering Lab in LA, it may have been Bernie Grundman or Doug Sax, but I am not sure. I was present but mostly silent. I loved to watch the process.

The three weeks flew by. Twelve tracks in the can. Now for the photo-shoot to create the LP cover. RCA hired a well-respected photographer, grammy winner, Gene Brownell, and he was superb to work with. The shoot took most of the day.

My cover idea was accepted by RCA, Frank Mulvey was the art director. I had provided my school picture from Bowker Vale School, Manchester, age six. I then put my 22-year-old head on each of the students' bodies with a different face, expression, and attire on each individual head. Some wore ribbons, some hair clips, some kids had glasses etc. I then left my 6-year-old head on my body to offer authenticity. Gene Brownell took two hundred shots to get the two dozen he needed. This was all done manually, pre-photoshop. On the back cover I put another picture of six-year-old Barry, and a report card from my teacher Mrs. Butterworth. The front cover was a blue sky, a sunrise, in the middle like the horizon, and a greenfield in the lower half.

'Blue Sky' was complete.

To introduce *Blue Sky* to the US market, RCA released *'Sweet America'*. The song was sent to US radio stations with little fanfare, but it was received well. Stations added it to playlists. In the first week it reached number 54, with a bullet, on the prestigious Billboard Chart. We were elated. RCA staff got out their sharpies and prepared a giant poster of a USA Map. Each major city was noted with a dot and its name. When the radio in that city, Cleveland, Fort Worth, etc. added the song, they placed a pin on the map. Each day it gained pins.

I came home to Vancouver in a state of bliss. Three weeks standing on the shoulder of giants. I had worked well with the best, held my own. RCA was ecstatic. Kershenbaum was thrilled. Barry was walking on clouds.

The cost incurred by RCA in 1973 for recording Blue Sky was US$38,000 in 1973 dollars. Using inflation at an average of 3.95% that translates to the LP costing $222,000 in 2025 dollars. A lot to invest in a new talent methinks. No clock ticking. RCA's motto was *'Let Barry create'*.

The wise owl John Lennon wrote in 'Beautiful Boy (Darling Boy)' *'Life is what happens to you while you're busy making other plans.'* A quote originally found in a 1957 Reader's Digest, written by Allen Saunders. John frequently found a way to share truth in a few words.

Life happened, the sun set, and the dark crept in. Thunder rolls.

On March 14th, 1973, John McCain along with 108 other US prisoners were released from the notorious Hanoi Hilton. McCain, the future Republican presidential candidate, and Senate Champion had been a prisoner of war in North Vietnam for five and a half years. This news was greeted with jubilation, coast to coast. The Maverick was home.

Kershenbaum called.

'US radio has banned *'Sweet America.'* We want you to fly to LA today'.

I was heading south, in a daze. The next two days I was in a room alone at RCA on the telephone. My job was to speak to Radio programmers in the US, and to explain to them that my song was not anti-American. The general retort I received after sixty plus calls was,

'Barry that is not the point. We are not playing any political music now. None!'

'Sweet America' was DOA. I cannot recall what I did or thought. Stunned I imagine. Then the other shoe dropped. Fred Ahlert called from NY.

'Barry, RCA are a problem. They will not agree to terms that I think are fair and necessary'.

To this day I do not know what RCA refused to provide Fred, but I can only guess that it was big money up front.

'I recommend that we move to another label and do a second LP taking all you have learnt from this experience. There is no shortage of offers'.

Fred was moving the goal posts. I was gobsmacked. My legs crumbled. My heart fluttered. Again, I cannot recall my response, or what transpired next in the conversation with Fred. Fred spoke in superlatives, even added that the sky was the limit.

Later that day, it was David Kershenbaum's time to call.

'Barry, RCA will not work with Fred Ahlert. We want you at RCA. Please let us help you. We can arrange the necessary lawyers to remove you from Fred's personal services contract. We will not work with Ahlert. We need you to decide what you will do. Separate from Ahlert and stay at RCA. But if you wish to continue with him as manager, we will be unable to proceed.

I cannot express the overwhelming fear, panic, and sadness that I felt that day. I am an anxious person. When I get faced with such a dilemma, I do not take flight, I do not fight, I freeze. I was awake in a nightmare.

I told David that my goal in life was to be a songwriter. That is what I said to Apple in 1968. Fred was a publisher. My pick was Fred Ahlert Jr. Song

writing over pop stardom. I repeat a phrase I wrote earlier in this chapter, which rang in my ears that day, Fred had told me, *'Barry you are the best lyricist I have met since Hal David.'*

It is extremely difficult for me to revisit and write about that day, 50 years ago. The heart is still connected. It is hard to revisit a loss. *'Blue Sky'* died on the vine. The life support was removed.

I separated from Fred Ahlert Jr. three months later. I learnt who the man was. A valuable lesson to remember.

Do I regret passing on Apple? No. Going back to university after *'The BBC Record of The Week'*? No. Choosing Fred over RCA? **Yes**! But hindsight is 20/20. Ob-La-Di, Ob-La-Da life goes on.

Blue Sky never got an official release. Early DJ and promotion copies, and some early pressings got out into the world. It is available today in used form on discogs etc. I do not really know the details, so I am unable to share.

Over the years I have received countless letters and emails from people,

'Barry your songs on Blue Sky have helped my wife as she was dealing with cancer.' 'Barry, we danced to your Blue-Sky songs at our wedding, 'Barry, I think Sweet America is an important political statement, thank you'.

Over the years people have surfaced who have stumbled onto *Blue Sky* and have shared words of love with me about the LP. It is always a wonderful gift to read and hear. Not a frequent event, but certainly a constant one.

Blue Sky is still a joy for me to visit in my headphones or playing the songs in concert. I describe the LP as an authentic example of seventies analogue sound, with heart-centered honest songs, and beautiful musicianship throughout. A wonderful time on my journey.

I have always enjoyed Bruce Springsteen's accurate observations of life. In his song *'Glory Days'* the Boss talks about the song's protagonist days of wonder. Days that he looks back at, smiles, as he gets strength and satisfaction from having lived. I have made music for all my life, six decades. '*Blue Sky*' was a period where it all worked. But they were not glory days. They were just good days.

As I have learnt from my wife Lori,
'*it's always meant to be the way it's meant to be!*'

Footnote:

Lately there has been a resurgence because Blue Sky has hit 50 years. Here are three examples:

One.... The Record Collector (a UK music magazine) featured Blue Sky in a three-page article in its June 2024 issue: 'Barry Greenfield might just be the

best songwriter you've probably never heard of. The English-born Canadian had a BBC Record of the Week back in 1970 with the Vietnam War protest

song "Sweet America", which also went to number one in England, followed by another number one in 1972 with "New York is Closed Tonight".

Two.... The Museum of Canadian Music honoured me by adding Blue Sky. The Museum, the largest Music internet presence in Canada (opened in 1988) wrote, 'Barry Greenfield's 1973 'Blue Sky', is one of the best Canadian albums ever recorded. Barry Greenfield made an important contribution to Canadian music.'

Three.... Dr. Bruce Lipton, PhD, cell biologist and lecturer, an internationally recognized leader in bridging science and spirit, wrote in his May 2024 Newsletter: 'Years of lecturing around this beautiful planet have provided me an opportunity to encounter wonderful Cultural Creatives that are helping to bring harmony into the world. I'd like to introduce you to a wonderful singer-songwriter and someone who I'm blessed to know, Barry Greenfield, who is celebrating the 50th anniversary of his RCA LP BLUE SKY'.

Discogs:
- *Great Folky Jazz Rock Album featuring Guitar Great Larry Carlton and other absolute top-notch session players.*

Here, Barry Greenfield at times channels Cat Stevens in a good way - Nice Stuff!

BLUE SKY TRACK LISTING and details.

A1   I'm On The Road To Safety

A2   Free The Lady

A3   How Long Can You Give Love

A4   Suicide

A5   Honey, Honey, Honey, Treat Me Nice

B1   New York Is Closed Tonight

B2   Concert Fever

B3   Milkman

B4   Sweet America

B5   Jack And Jill

B6   My Last Blues

Companies, etc.
- Pressed By – RCA Records Pressing Plant, Indianapolis
- Mastered At – The Mastering Lab

Credits
- Arranged By – Jimmie Haskell and Barry Greenfield
- Art Direction – Frank Mulvey

12.
- Backing Vocals [Background] – Brooks Hunnicutt (tracks: A4), Daniel J. Moore* (tracks: A1)
- Bass – Joe Osborn
- Cover, Photography By – Gene Brownell
- Drums – Jim Gordon (tracks: B1, B2, B3, B4), Russ Kunkel (tracks: A1, A2, A3, A4, A5, B5, B6)
- Engineer – Peter Abbott*, Rick Ruggieri
- Guitar – Deam Parks (tracks: B1, B2, B3, B4)
- Keyboards – Larry Knechtel (tracks: A5, B5, B6), Larry Muhoberac (tracks: A1, A2, A3, A4, B1, B2, B3, B4)
- Lead Guitar – Larry Carlton
- Percussion – Gene Estes (tracks: B1, B2, B3, B4), Milt Holland (tracks: A2, A5, B4, B5, B6)
- Producer – David M Kershenbaum *
- Remix, Engineer – Brian Christian, Rick Ruggieri
- Written-By, Vocals, Acoustic Guitar – Barry Greenfield

Notes
Pressed with Orange RCA Dynaflex Labels

Larry Carlton Appears Courtesy of Blue Thumb Records
Barcode and Other Identifiers
- Matrix / Runout (Side A Runout Etched): APL 1-0264 A 2S
- Matrix / Runout (Side A Runout Stamped): TML I A1
- Matrix / Runout (Side B Runout Etched): APL 1-0264 B 2S
- Matrix / Runout (Side B Runout Stamped): I A 1
- Rights Society: BMI

BLUE SKY DELUXE EDITION 2024
https://open.spotify.com/playlist/6J5WRfLdnXcSEvd0waMt67?si=a472c790e77641af

https://open.spotify.com/playlist/6J5WRfLdnXcSEvd0waMt67?si=a472c790e77641af

8

The afternoon that I met Harry Nilsson and Richard Starkey 1973

It was 10am, Thursday, day nine. My destination was Studio 'B'. I flew past security; the guards all knew me. *'g' morning Barry!'* Home-made posters were hanging everywhere. Handwritten, prepared by the RCA staff, using various coloured sharpies. They read, *'WELCOME RINGO!'*, *'WE LOVE YOU RINGO!'*. Entering Studio B (smaller than 'A', as is the tradition), I asked my producer David Kershenbaum.

'What's going on with all these posters hanging everywhere?'

David was as excited as me (In 1973 he was as starstruck as I was. It was early days for us both).

'Harry Nilsson is recording all day in Studio 'A'. Security advised everyone that Ringo Starr is planning a visit.'

'A' was a few steps away.

Nilsson? I loved everything he did. His writing. His vocals. His ideas. His originality. John Lennon described Harry as his favourite American artist. I agreed. *'Spaceman,' 'Coconut,' 'Without You,' 'Jump into the Fire'*. The list of great songs written, and sung, by Nilsson was endless. Plus, wonderful production. Harry had it all.

The Hoffman-Voight movie, *'Midnight Cowboy'* was where the world was introduced to Nilsson. *'Everybody's Talkin'* (Echoes)' rode through the film. This Fred Neil song was the perfect beast. Words, chords, melody, all married. Written in 1966 and recorded by Harry in 1969. The films director rejected a Harry song, *'I Guess the Lord Must Live in New York City'* and picked this Fred Neil song. Lucky Harry, he still got to sing it. That's the music business in a bottle. A simple twist of fate! A career was born. It was Harry's vocal interpretation that kicked it out of the stadium. I recall comparing it to John Lennon's vocals on, from *'With the Beatles'*, *'You Really Got a Hold On Me,'* a Smokey Robinson treasure. It sent chills through me. As my wife often says, *'it gives me goosebumps'*.

I believe that interpretation in a cover song is an art. Few have it. A second example of such a cover is Sinead O'Connor singing Prince's' powerful, *'Nothing Compares 2 U'*. Another is *'You're No Good'*, performed by Linda Ronstadt. Linda was helped with a strong production by Peter Asher, and by my friend, Andrew Gold, who played most of the instruments on that classic song. All of these great moments in recorded music have another aspect in common, unique story lines, an integral component.

Distracted by the electricity in the air, Nilsson in 'A', I kept my focus, as I entered *the coal mine*. I took my seat next to Kershenbaum and we began the days work. The song on the menu was a favourite of mine, *'Jack and Jill'*. Wednesday, we had recorded the basic track, and it shone bright. Larry Carlton, and me, guitars; Joe Osborn, bass; Milt Holland, percussion; and Larry Knechtel, from Bread, (and the pianist on *'Bridge Over Troubled Water)'*, on the keyboards. The final step, before recording my vocal, was to add an accordion, the needed colour. I wanted to bring a Parisienne feel to the song. Larry Muhoberac was given the task, *'pour que ça ressemble à Paris'*. The lyric was nursery rhyme in approach, *'oh wow, gee whiz, the world moved, it was their first kiss, and that ballroom became such a small room'*. I liked the lightness of the tune.

At 11.30 am nature called. Upon walking into the loo, I find that I was not alone. Harry Nilsson was sitting on a black leather stool next to the shelf that ran below the mirrors. Smiling at me.

I'm a shy guy, and I froze. In his right hand he held a small silver spoon. In his left, a small plastic bag with powder in it. That really freaked me out. I had never been in the company of a criminal drug. I'm not the bravest of dudes. I may be naïve, but I knew from watching the movie *Serpico*, that that bag was not talcum powder, it was cocaine. The small silver spoon was my confirmation. Music Industry reality 101.

'Hi'.

'Hello!' I replied.

'I'm Harry, who are you? Want some? A groupie laid it on me outside the building?'

'Mmm, Thanks but no thanks!'

I'd better answer. *'I'm Barry Greenfield. I'm working in Studio 'B'*, I stuttered.

Its always weird when two men chat in a bathroom. We both know that we are there to relieve ourselves. Harry had different motives. Someone can walk in, but it still offers a certain privacy, sometimes, a brief warm couple of sentences happen. I relieved myself. Then he filled his silver spoon, and he did it. Once in the left, once in the right. I washed my hands. I was not relaxed. Harry wanted to talk. So, me and Nilsson chatted for ten minutes. It seemed unimportant that we were in a small corporate men's room.

He looked just like Harry. He sounded just like Harry. He was kind, friendly, open, and normal. I relaxed more. Things concluded with Harry saying,

'If you have time, come into 'A' and help me with the mix.' He was gone.

'Help him with the mix?'

I ran back to 'B'. Shared my story. Kershenbaum listened to my tale and quickly, emphatically said,

'Go, go, go! We'll finish the accordion without you. Don't pass up such an opportunity Barry'.

I went. I did not waffle.

I knocked on the door of 'A' like you would a neighbour's front door. I walked in, he invited me to sit in the large leather mix chair to his left. We spent two hours working on a Harry track. I played with the gain, the EQ, the auxiliary sends, the pan, the volume, the reverb levels; I learnt a great deal that day from Harry. Two hours full of classroom.

The song was from the movie he had making with Ringo Starr, *'Son of Dracula,'* a musical, from Apple Films, released the following year, 1974, to no aplomb. Harry was working on the film's soundtrack. Again, no aplomb.

It was amazing hearing the great sounds pop out of the huge speakers in 'A'. He had extremely talented players on the track. Harry was mixing the only new song for the films soundtrack, *'Daybreak'*, the others were taken from his LPs. Harry told me that he recorded the song in London at Trident Studios. Joining Nilsson and Starr was Klaus Voormann, Peter Frampton, and George Harrison, who played the cowbell. The names he dropped made me shiver. I requested to hear the cowbell part isolated. Harry laughed and gave me ten seconds.

Harry let me work the board a little, and seemed genuinely interested, as he listened to input from me, and the engineer to his right. Harry spent a long time working on the bass guitar, Voormann, and the kick drum, Starr, marrying them, both in the sound spectrum and selecting correct volumes and reverb for each. I watched, I learnt, and it is something I do to this day in my mixing. He would occasionally refresh his nose, but never seemed *out of control*. Time flew by. I grew more at ease.

Until the world's axis reversed on its spin. At 2pm the door swung open. The magic of that Thursday was about to dissolve. In a nano-second.

In walked Ringo Starr and Richard Perry (Harry and Ringo's record producer back in the day). Ringo had a bottle of Jack Daniels, half-full, in his left hand. He passed it to Harry, who took a chug. Then to Richard Perry, he chugged too. I was not included. No one thought to offer the kid a chug.

I rose from my honoured seat left of Harry and went to the chair behind. That original seat sat empty. Ringo and Richard stood. Harry was thrilled at the arrival of his mates. It was lovely to feel and see. They chatted about the confusion in the RCA parking lot. I was ignored. I felt like the invisible man.

I have read the same story from others, who have experienced similar events. Apparently, this happens whenever any Beatle enters any room. Eric Clapton once said that in 1967 he was a huge presence in London. People used to call him *'god'*, for heavens sake. But when he went with George Harrison anywhere, every time, he became invisible to all, George took all the eyes. This may be true when the Pope walks into a room. I doubt Madonna has that affect. Taylor Swift might? Tom Brady? Cristiano Ronaldo? Diana, surely.

I was quiet, I was ignored, I felt uneasy. At long last Harry turned to me and said,

'Richard Starkey this is Barry Greenberg.'

I did not correct Harry's error. He repeated the same intro with Richard Perry. Barry Greenberg I was. Ringo smiled and shook my hand. Perry nodded. I never left my chair. Frozen and feeling somewhat lost. The opposite being the case when it was just Harry.

The three lads passed the Daniels from hand to hand. The two late arrivals were drunk, loud, and inappropriate for the church-like environment that is a control room in a studio. Harry took out his plastic bag, and all three imbibed the substance. Party time 2pm, Pacific. The engineer was silent. I was not alone. There were two distinct cliques. The elite, Harry, Richard and Ringo, and the mere mortals. The A group were stoned, and pissed, the B's were watching, silently, carefully.

Richard Starkey appeared tired and wasted. Scruffy and English. He sounded like the man from *A Hard Day's Night*. The lanky, six foot four, Richard Perry looked like a good fit for these two. He was with his artists, and these were his glory days. It would not continue for much longer. Soon both Ringo and Harry changed their producer. Perry went on to work on '*Stand Tall*' with Burton Cummings.

It was time to leave. (I can sense these things). I thanked Harry, bigtime; shook his hand. No hugs. I smiled at his friends.

Barry Greenberg the invisible one, blown-away to be a yard from Richard Starkey, my favourite drummer, ever! Harry looked my way kindly and with warmth. I was a happy camper. I went back to my safe place, my home in 'B'. We finished the accordion part on 'Jack and Jill.' My partners in crime in 'B' wanted all the details. I gave them a recap. My journal entry that night took an hour, or more.

I became much smarter as a recording guy because of Harry Nilsson. He really understood music. A giant of a talent, and he was a wonderful person to me.

Nilsson died of heart failure on January 15, 1994, in his Agoura Hills, California, home at the age of 52. When I hear his LPs' now, I float back to that afternoon. It altered the rudder. If you change the rudder half a degree, you end up somewhere else! I loved every second in Studio A with Harry, and I became aware that Ringo was unique to all others......that was '*The Day I met Harry Nilsson.*'

Footnote:

Will Jennings wrote a great lyric for Stevie Winwood, 'While you see a chance, take it'. If a door opens walk through it. A chance does not always pay, but when it does it can be brilliant.

I could have avoided studio 'A' and allowed 'shy Barry' to win. But I dug deep and stood up and walked into the unknown. I am thankful I did.

Courage is rewarded.

Often, I hear an athlete, or an artist who wins a prestigious award say to the audience, 'I am blessed, and so too are you. I got here by using my gift and hard work. You can do that too. Don't stop dreaming, keep on working.'

It is not about the destination; it is about the journey.

MANCHESTER SCHOOL, AGE 6, 1956. *Barry top row second from left with blazer.*

Barry in London, Apple visit July 1968

Prior to Apple audition, 1968

Barry and John Lee Hooker at Saskatoon hotel on Canadian tour 1972.

*Barry Greenfield with 10cc
"Sweet America"
BBC RECORD OF THE WEEK
1970.*

Barry in jeans in Chinatown 1973

CKWX Radio Interview 1972

Barry on plane on tour 1972

Barry in Seattle at Pike Place Market 1973

On the road with band, 1972

RCA BLUE SKY Front Cover 1973

RCA BLUE SKY Back Cover 1973

BLUE SKY Side A

BLUE SKY Side B

Live with Supertramp 1974 Vancouver Queen Elizabeth Theatre

Harold Moon Socan award
'outstanding contribution
to Canadian Music" 1972

NEW YORK IS CLOSED
Canadian single 1972

RCA Single NEW YORK IS
CLOSED TONIGHT 1973

Second LP
SANCTUARY 1974

CANADA SKY
Single 1974

Barry Greenfield EXPOSED SOUL CD Nashville May 2008

Greenfield
Greyhound
GAYE
DELORME

Hat pic 2007

Rehearsing with Chris Nole in Nashville 2010

Family in Paris 2018

Shane Fontayne and Barry, Tarrytown NY 2016.    *Graham Nash Poster Tarrytown NY 2016.*

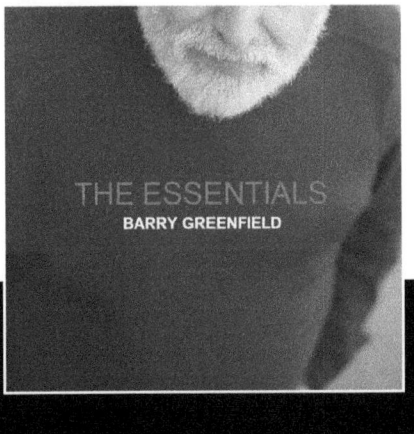

ESSENTIALS
2018
Front Cover

Barry Greenfield Quartet 2018

At Home, 2020

Barry and Gurian guitar 2025.

Yad Vashem book cover 2022

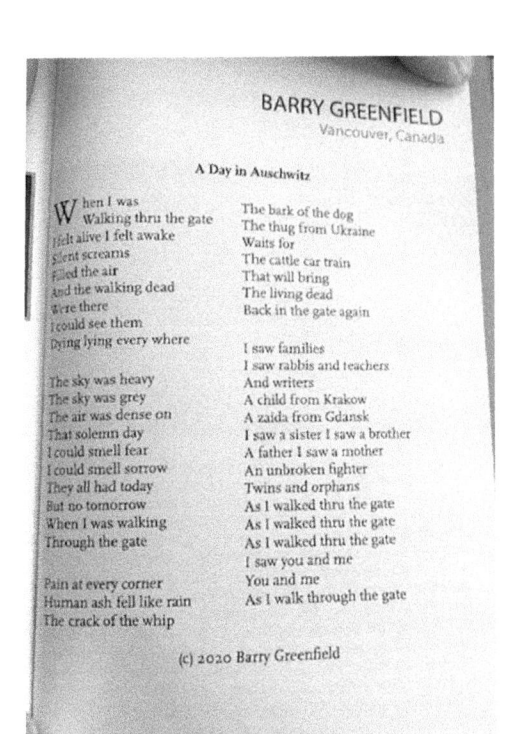

A Day in Auschwitz

When I was
Walking thru the gate
I felt alive I felt awake
Silent screams
Filled the air
and the walking dead
Were there
I could see them
Dying lying every where

The sky was heavy
The sky was grey
The air was dense on
That solemn day
I could smell fear
I could smell sorrow
They all had today
But no tomorrow
When I was walking
Through the gate

Pain at every corner
Human ash fell like rain
The crack of the whip

The bark of the dog
The thug from Ukraine
Waits for
The cattle car train
That will bring
The living dead
Back in the gate again

I saw families
I saw rabbis and teachers
And writers
A child from Krakow
A zaida from Gdansk
I saw a sister I saw a brother
A father I saw a mother
An unbroken fighter
Twins and orphans
As I walked thru the gate
As I walked thru the gate
As I walked thru the gate
I saw you and me
You and me
As I walk through the gate

(c) 2020 Barry Greenfield

BARRY GREENFIELD
Vancouver, Canada

THE GATE lyric,
Yad Vashem coffee table book page 51

2025.

*Gurian Brazilian Rosewood Guitar that I bought in 1970.
I wrote every song on this instrument after that.*

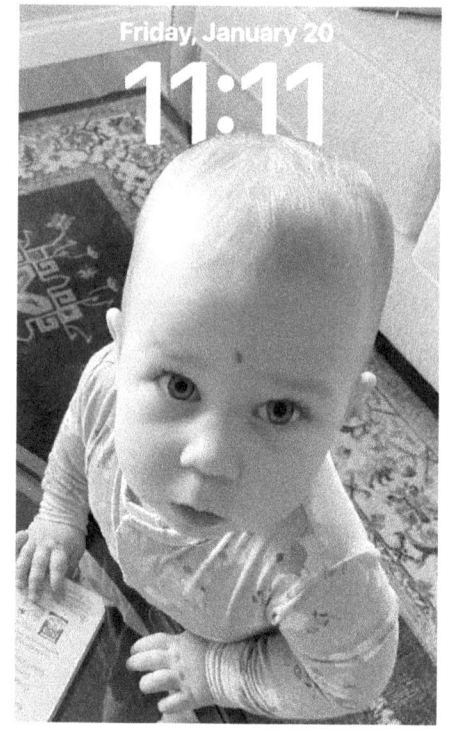

Lil Angel *Littlest Angel*

Wedding dance kids

Lori Greenfield

Wife and husband

9

Thanksgiving dinner at Mike Nesmith's Home 1973

Twenty-two, no serious relationship, shy, and wide-eyed. A period where I am creative. Writing many songs, not all keepable, but that's the process that is mine. I was working in the City of Angels, on my LP *'Blue Sky'*. I was growing, learning and enjoying every moment of my Hollywood experience. Then out of the blue I received a dinner invite. It became an evening to remember. An old friend called early that morning to ask me to join him for Thanksgiving dinner at Monkee Mike Nesmith's mansion, 4pm. This evening would prove to be insightful, fun, and scary too. The soiree ended at 3am with an epiphany that affected many decisions henceforth. But that night to remember, was still six hours away.

It was 10am when I walked into the control room to find my new friend, and guitarist extraordinaire, Larry Carlton waiting, with a smile and a black coffee in his left hand, that he had poured for me. Our discussions frequently went deep in these early LA mornings. That day we focused on history, November 22nd, 1963, the day that JFK was assassinated, and LBJ was sworn in as the 36th President.

Here we sat in 'B' a full decade later, it was November 22nd, 1973. Two history buffs, reliving the horror of that tragedy. We discussed the details, and its long-lasting aftermath. This moment etched in time, created a paler shade of grey that hung over the studio. The mood slightly shifted, when we recalled how The Beatles helped heal the Nation a few months later, singing *'I Want to Hold your Hand'*. Larry and I sang the song's bridge in unison, a cappella.

The day trundled along without incident. We had a great track finished for *'Milkman'*. We flowed smoothly like the Nile. I was adlibbing my finest John Cleese impression, to add as a Monty Python homage to the songs tag, *'good morning Mrs. Sim, having a lovely day? Hubby be gone by ten? Manchester United 3 Tottenham Hotspur 1. See you then!'*

The engineer, Peter Abbott, came into my headphones. *'Barry your guest has arrived'*.

My DJ friend who worked in LA radio, Peter Starr, was at security seeking entry. It was Peter who had invited me to join him for Thanksgiving dinner at the Beverley Hills home of Monkee Mike Nesmith. Luckily, we finished early due to the holiday.

The sun was high in the blue Californian sky. It was 4pm and we are driving down Sunset Boulevard in a British sports car, a 1965 MG, bright red. Starr in the driving seat, me the clueless navigator. Soon we were idling in front of a closed twelve-foot-tall iron gate. Peter spoke into the intercom that waited beside the gate.

'Mike its Peter and Barry.'

A voice came out of the box. It had a Texan drawl. It was Mike Nesmith from the weekly NBC TV show that I had watched and enjoyed years ago.

'I'll open the gate. Don't get out of the car until I come out!' was the instruction.

We drove up the winding road to a flat area outside a four-car garage. A sign nailed on the garage door, '**DO NOT LEAVE CAR UNTIL GREETED.**' We obeyed.

I was a teenager when the TV series and the hit singles were being made. The Monkees filmed 58 episodes. Tork left in 1968. Nesmith in 1970. However, the Monkees continued to reform, and perform, in various combinations of, two, three or four members for the ensuing decades. Mike was my favourite Monkee.

Their songs, I refer only to the *hits*, were extraordinarily strong. But they came from the pianos and pens of Tommy Boyce and Bobby Hart (*'Last train to Clarksville'*), Carole King and Gerry Goffin (*'Pleasant Valley Sunday'*) and Neil Diamond (*'I'm a Believer'*).

When one gets the rare opportunity to share an evening with *the important Monkee*, you say *'Thank You.'* I had no idea what lay ahead, held my breath, closed my eyes and I walked through door number three.

Outside the sprawling bungalow, Starr and I sat in the red MG, two doors locked, roof up. The presence of a mountainous German shepherd circling the car with bad intent made me think of a train platform, *'Judenramp'*.

Mike walked out. A tall fellow, wearing the famous Monkee green touk from the series, (I kid you not!). Mike spoke, gave a command to his dog in

German. The dog sat, still panting like they do, always looking like they had just run a marathon. Mike asked us to get out of the car. Peter and I were petrified. We shook hands, smiled, and walked in. My heart beating, Peter looked shaken. With the giant dog in tow, we entered Nesmith's beautiful home.

It was luxurious, but still comfortable. Three soft couches; light-coloured carpets; lamps on; candles, photographs of Texas and geography. No Monkee memorabilia; all American no European or Asian design. I loved it.

Mike offered us a drink. Mike was working on a beer of his own. Peter took a beer. Me a cola. Our host was gracious, considerate, and sincere. A lovely man. *The short tour* was offered, escorted by the King of six thousand square feet.

Joanne walked in. Joanne was quiet and reserved. Mike was gregarious and not reserved. Joanne was petite, Mike was huge. After sharing space with them for an hour they seemed like two bookends, unmatched, but they kept the books in order and in place. Mike wrote a wonderful song called '*Joanne*' in 1970.

'Her name was Joanne, and she lived in a meadow by a pond. And she touched me for a moment, with a look that spoke to me of her sweet love.'

We chatted for a bit. No staff, Joanne was on kitchen duty, Mike was not. At about 6pm we moved to the dining room table that was laid out for

Thanksgiving. American theme. Red, white, and blue. I remember that the salt and pepper shakers were in the US in theme too. Stars and stripes. The meal was served. Main course first. We had turkey, mashed potatoes, carrots, and smorgasbord of delicious sides. Pickles, sauces, olives. Wine was poured. I drank water.

Mike and I were both British Invasion devotees. We both knew lots of the trivia about the lyrics, artists, and recordings of that period 1964-1969. Troggs, Peter and Gordon, Stones, The Beatles, The Outsiders, The Kinks, Paul Revere, and the Raiders. Our two colleagues chimed in from time to time. The room had the feeling of a Tuesday trivia night at the pub, the topic '*Sixties Bands.*'

We ate slowly. Pumpkin pie was the finale. Soon after a second, then a third wine bottle appeared, the last plate was removed, I helped Joanne with cleaning up, but she drew the line on my offer to dry the dishes. Mike and Peter retreated to the living room. Mike efficiently opened the third bottle of red. I know a little more about wine now, *une petite quantité de connaissances,* but in those early days all I knew was it came in red or white.

Without an announcement Joanne entered the room with a tray that could have been used for Brooke Bond tea and crumpets, but clearly was not. Mike said,

'*some more deserts gentlemen.*'

The room shifted. An uncomfortable vibe entered. Peter and my surprised look was obvious to our hosts, but we attempted to play it '*cool.*' Mike explained to us the smorgasbord on the tray, hashish, quaaludes, and other words I forget, names that I had never heard before, or since, Mike described them as a thanksgiving treat. They were neatly spaced, filling the tea tray. Alongside the hashish, and a small pipe, were various coloured, multi-sized pills, all laid out like a selection of macarons in a Parisian café.

First, the couple smoked hash in a small clay pipe, Peter and I passed, as they constantly replaced the herb in the pipe's small bowl. Nice smell I thought. Then they moved on, to select from the various coloured pills. Discussing the potential combinations, like two *chefs de cuisine* in a Brooklyn kitchen, they chose from the generous collection of uppers, downers and whatever. It reminded me of a tray of antipasto, the traditional first course of a formal Italian meal. Bite-size small portions, presented on a platter, from which everyone serves themselves. The slight tension that was ever-present slowly lifted, as Joanne and Mike's normal energy was lightened by the arrival of their *medication of choice.* An hour slipped by. Conversations remained normal. Topics unchanged, varied, and fun. We all participated in the chat, Peter drank another beer, and I drank coffee made by Joanne.

The hash haze hung over the room. We all must have had a contact high. Mike jumped up. Energized. Mike, the ringmaster directed us all to the music room. The three males walked into his music-cave. Joanne went through another doorway. We never saw her again. She wanted privacy, and I imagine, sleep.

The cave was impressive. Walls adorned with gold Monkee LP's and singles. Memorabilia from years gone by. Guitars strewn around. A 12 string, a Gibson, a Tele, a Rickenbacker like Lennons'. A bass. A Ludwig drum kit in the rear. Mike explained a bit about his memorabilia that he thought would be interesting. It was. A *'Last Train to Clarksville'* gold record; framed pictures of Mike and Ringo, Mike and John; posters advertising Monkee Live shows in California. His references to his band were always delivered in a condescending negative form. Later that evening he went deeper into his anger and embarrassment at *being a Monkee*. I found this to be sad, understandable, but still sad. I was a stranger, so it struck me as *'private and personal'* and therefore inappropriate to share with me. The Monkees had some great hits. 'Stepping Stone', *'Daydream Believer'*, *'Pleasant Valley Sunday'*. But by 1973 music had evolved. Elton had arrived. Wings were here. *'Tapestry'*, *'Dark Side of the Moon'*, *'Harvest'*.

Then out-of-the-blue Mike handed me an old Gibson acoustic. A beauty.

'Barry, play me something you wrote,' Mike asked.

I played him *'New York is Closed Tonight'*. He smiled. For the next hour, or more, we bounced back and forth. He played a Nesmith song; I played a Greenfield song. Then we morphed into Beatle tunes. *'Norwegian Wood'*,

'Yes, it Is', *'Help'*, *'Do You Want to Know a Secret?'* I recall playing the Stones' *'Play with Fire,'* which I taught him. He knew a lot of the words to *'Mr. Tambourine Man'* and he sang it great. But the highlight for me was his wonderful acoustic version of *'Joanne.'* She had been long gone by now, but I knew she was upstairs somewhere. I requested *'Different Drum'* the song he wrote that was covered by Linda Ronstadt and the Stone Poneys and got to #12 on Billboard. He nailed it. Mike explained to me that he had offered the song to The Monkees, who had rejected it. I thought he sounded hurt by that rejection. It is such a fabulous song. They should have sung that gem.

I really enjoyed this part of the night. He was a gifted writer, player, and singer. Funny too. Stoned as he must have been, and perhaps a little drunk too, he always appeared present and alert. He was in tune, and I was in sync. The pills and hash kept visiting. Peter fell asleep on a couch. It was just me and Mike. I was not tired at all. It was a night to remember.

Mike had purchased this house with '*Monkee-Money.*' Mike repeated that the Monkees embarrassed him, and that he wanted to make '*good music.*' He felt that he was being overpaid as a Monkee, and that he could perform at a much higher level as a solo. He told me that he was leaving tomorrow afternoon to go to San Francisco to play a 'silly-Monkee-reunion' show, a one-nighter, and coming home with $10,000.

Why was he *so naked* with me? The pills? The hash? We felt like we were equal that night, but we were not. I was unknown, he was recognized wherever he went. He had enough in the bank to feel no stress about the phone bill. I was not that blessed. But who was happier? I was excited for the future; Mike seemed unhappy, not in control, a man uncomfortable in his suit.

Fame has always intrigued me. Beatlemania was scary. The Lads were in the eye of the hurricane. Loving it but hating it. In Manila, 1966, it could have ended tragically for the Boys. The Marcos's believed that the group snubbed the First Family. There were violent scenes at Manila airport.

Mike talked in detail about his sadness and discomfort with Monkee fame, suggesting that it was somehow not earned. By 11pm we had exhausted our repertoire. But this memorable and unique evening with Mike Nesmith had one last chapter.

Mike told me how he had bought this house a year earlier from Glen Campbell. I was in Glen's old house. I imagined that one of my favourite songwriters, Jimmy Webb, may have played that grand piano, '*Wichita Lineman,* '*By the Time I get to Phoenix*', '*Galveston*', that now sat dormant in the foyer.

With Joanne nowhere to be seen, and Peter crashed on a couch, me and Mike headed out to his pool. We were not at the pool to swim. It was 1am so no sunbathing. Mike wanted to play Beatles records. Specifically, '*Paperback Writer.*' He played the Capitol Records 45 '*Paperback Writer*' on an expensive state of the art sound system, perhaps 20 times. Under Mike's direction, we focused on the Paul McCartney bass part. Sitting by his pool, side-by-side in twin shell chairs. Each chair had two speakers, level with each ear. A right stereo channel, and a left.

This is *'real music Barry.'* I agreed.

A Beatle recording, on quality speakers, on a quality system. Like good cognac. I was incredibly happy to share The Beatles with another aficionado. Mike Nesmith. A Monkee.

The recording of Paul's *'Paperback Writer'* is marked by the boosted bass guitar sound. Geoff Emerick the Beatles' recording engineer for *Revolver*, later said: *'Paperback Writer' was the first time the bass sound had been heard in all its grandeur. Paul played a different bass, a Rickenbacker. Then we boosted it further by using a loudspeaker as a microphone. Paul and I positioned it directly in front of Paul's bass speaker and the moving diaphragm of the second speaker made the electric current.'* McCartney's playing was also more melodic and busier than on previous tracks.

Nesmith loved that trick of the tail. It sounded unworldly good.

We had grown tired and talked out. Like Cinderella I had to go. I woke Peter up. Mike walked us to the car. We hugged goodbye, like two friends, two hippies. *What a night!*

I was back in my room at the Holiday Inn. Back at work in 'B' again in a few hours. What I did not know was that I was about to meet Nilsson, and Ringo, that afternoon.

Footnote:

Lying in my hotel king bed I thought about my night, and how fame was embedded in all Nesmith did. Looking back now I realize that:

For all the houses, all the suites, and all the limousines, that Nesmith, Bowie, Cher, Harrison, and Jagger had found, there are many who entered the game and found a different result. A painful truth.

Some saw it fade like English fog. One hit wonders.

Some literally fell to earth from the sky, Buddy Holly, Stevie Ray Vaughan, John Denver.

Some overdosed too young chasing dragons, John Bonham, Cass Elliot, Nick Drake, Jimi Hendrix, and The Who's legendary drummer, Keith Moon.

Others ended abruptly, Kurt Cobain, Chris Cornell, Elliot Smith.

Some were broken. Badfinger, Michael Hutchence, Janis Joplin.

Much like when Malorie Hayes floated in a rowboat down the Smith River, in the film 'Birdbox'. I too was floating downstream. Onboard my raft without a paddle, I had my lyrics, my music, and my dreams.

The musical river that I have sailed down had brought marvelous moments. Occasionally they arrived like unsuspected rapids; frequently, they were unpredictable, like ocean waves. ***At rare times, these moments resulted in an epiphany.*** *One such epiphany came on November 22nd, 1973, in Mike Nesmith's home. An epiphany brighter than a thousand suns.*

Mike had it all. Home, partner, instruments, talent, health. But I watched him escape into a haze, and a fog, of hash, alcohol, and pills. He never kissed Joanne. Never spoke a loving word or shot a sweet glance in her direction. She was the same with Mike. The beautiful Beverly Hills house was not a home it was a building. Vacant of love, and void of joy. Just expensive toys and nice furniture.

'Is that all there is?'

10

The songwriter's triangle, Joni, Buffy and me 1974

"Do not judge me by my success, judge me by how many times I fell down and got back up again." – Nelson Mandela

Somehow, somewhere, I found the inner fortitude, which I needed to keep on keeping on. If I did not take steps, forward motion would cease. When a pond is still, not moving, it becomes stagnant.

I began the recording of my second LP. I wanted to self produce, and I chose Heart's studio in Vancouver. I had twenty strong songs ready, arranged, and complete. I signed a one off deal with Casino Records, a Canadian Independent Label. They paid all the recording costs.

I hired the best Canadian Musicians. People I had worked with over the last three years. Robbie King, piano, Duris Maxwell, kit, Ken Lundgren bass, Terry Frewer guitar, Doug Edwards guitar, Claire Lawrence, sax, harmonica, and confidant. The LP, *'Sanctuary'* took two months, and was very organic. A positive experience on all levels. Recorded in Vancouver with Rolf Henneman on the board, but improved, and mixed by Tom Vicari in LA. David Campbell (Beck's Dad) wrote the string arrangements in Hollywood. I played the centrepiece role on my guitars, and I urged these great free form players to feel their parts. It was more Grateful Dead than Jim Croce. I wanted to paint a different picture on my second outing. A lesson that The Beatles left in their legacy for all musicians. Grow, take risks, evolve!

The first single *'Canada Sky'* zoomed to number one in Canada. The LP sold steady. I continued playing many live concerts in all types of venues. I was growing as a player and enjoying writing different songs. Band songs and solo songs. I had a few artists record Greenfield songs.

I was feeling good about my art, and by happenstance I had a conversation with Joni Mitchell's manager Sam Feldman, in a local eatery. I had known Sam since I was a teenager. He was a leading figure in the Canadian Music Scene and was happy to hear about my latest adventures. During the thirty-minute exchange with Sam the conversation morphed into our chatting about his client Joni. He told me that Joni was very happy with her new home in Sechelt, British Columbia. Sechelt was a three-hour drive from my home in Kitsilano, a lovely daytrip, which included a ferry portion, and lots of beauty.

When I walked out of the RCA Building in LA the staff had presented me with a box of shrink-wrapped copies of *'Blue Sky'*, twenty-five in total. I gave copies of the LP to family, friends and neighbours. I had a few left in my bedroom closet. I thought, I would love to gift one to Joni Mitchell. I would give a sealed copy to Joni, after all music is to share. Canada post was out, I had no address. I decided to drive to Sechelt, locate her home, and drop a pristine copy of *'Blue Sky'* off. Let the adventure begin.

My *bat-mobile* was a 1962 two-tone-green Austin Cambridge that I had purchased for $200. My first car. I prayed she would make the trip without incident. Joni's copy of *'Blue Sky'* was sitting, waiting, sleeping, on the passenger seat, I left home at sunrise to catch the BC Ferry to Gibsons and then drive down the road to Lund. Joni had built her home at Half-Moon Bay, near Lund, and Sam Feldman had given me the road map I would need,

'If you drive the Lund road, you will arrive at a rock that is painted by Joni. A beautiful collection of bright rainbow colours. It was painted as a road-sign for her visitors.'

This is her signpost.

'At the painted rock, turn left, then drive down the gravel road to the stone house at the end of the driveway'.

The ferry ride was peaceful, very green, very blue. The Sunshine Coast Road was winding and slow. After an hour of driving, suddenly, much like a lighthouse on a foggy night, I saw my signpost. The rock that was painted by Joni Mitchell. It was four foot high, two feet wide. Joni had painted a lady's face on it. Long hair, flowers, all in inviting bright colours, just as Feldman had described. I turned left and drove down the one lane dirt-path.

After one hundred yards the gravel road turned to grass, rough grass, not pristine lawn. There sat a beautiful, small, rock house. A stone domicile, at the end of the driveway, the Sechelt home of Joni Mitchell. I turned off the engine, sat for a minute to calibrate, then with *'Blue Sky'* in hand I walked to the solid, numberless, wooden-front-door and I knocked. No reply. I knocked again expecting the same, when,

'Hello', can I help you?'

I turned to see a man in a winter coat and English cap smiling at me. He seemed to appear out of nowhere.

'Yes, please I'm looking for Joni.'

'I'm her caretaker, and Joni is in LA. Not sure when she'll be back'.

I stood there unsure what to say. He saw the LP in my left hand.

This man was intuitive and kind. I have never met Joni, but her music speaks volume about her life. This fellow was open and smiling yet I could sense that he was protective of his tenant. He looked me deeply in the eyes, standing a yard away from me, read my energy, and trust arrived.

'If you want to leave something for Joni, she gets all her mail at the pub, 'The Lighthouse.' It's a few miles back. If you leave it there, she'll get it when she gets back to Sechelt'.

I thanked him for his kindness. He pointed to a large flat, couch-sized boulder, suggesting I sit there and enjoy the peace before the long-drive back to Vancouver. I went to where he pointed and sat quietly on that beautiful seat enjoying the wind, the water, the silence, nature. My perch was beside the open ocean.

The man vanished. Much as he had appeared. Abruptly and without fanfare. I did not know where he came from, or where he went. He literally appeared and then he disappeared. It is entirely possible that I could have driven half a day to Half Moon Bay, found a closed door, with no mail slot, and would have returned to Vancouver mission not accomplished. If he had not been present in that moment of time, part two of this tale, may not have occurred.

Twenty yards from my rock-seat, were a cluster of rocks sitting above the water line. I recognized that these rocks were the ones that Joni stood on, naked, in the gatefold picture in her LP *'For the Roses.'* The story that I heard in LA about that artwork was illuminating. It seems that Joni presented the label, Asylum

Records, with a full-rear nude photograph of herself standing on these ocean rocks, as her choice for the front cover of that LP. The label President, David Geffen, vetoed the naked picture. Geffen wanted her face on the cover.

'For the Roses' was released in November 1972, between her two biggest commercial and critical successes, *'Blue'* and *'Court and Spark'*, but Asylum, a supposedly *'artist-oriented label'*, did not use the cover that the artist wanted. I thought how strange, that the record label could select the picture that they felt would sell the product better, Joni's face, and that they would ignore the wishes of an artist of Joni Mitchell's stature. I found that unsettling. Not surprising, just music business reality.

Wishing farewell to the waters edge, the stone home, and the ghostlike caretaker, I climbed back into my two-tone green Austin Cambridge, which started easily, another success. I headed back to Gibsons and my ferryboat.

I stopped at the pub, *'The Lighthouse'*, as directed by the caretaker, leaving the sealed copy of *'Blue Sky'* with the barkeep. Taped onto the cover a short note of explanation for Joni. He told me that she was unpredictable, and that she may not pick up her mail for months. That was in 1974, and the next fourteen years went by without any response from Ms. Mitchell.

In spring 1988, the next chapter in this tale began. The phone rang. Many of my exciting musical phone calls arrive on a Sunday. Fred Ahlert Jr. David Sancious. John Lee Hooker. This time it was Buffy Sainte-Marie.

'Hello is this Barry Greenfield?'
'Yes'.
'It's Buffy Wolfchild'.
'Sorry, I don't know who you are.'
'It's Buffy Sainte-Marie', came the reply. (Wolfchild was her real name).

That name I knew. Buffy had recorded two of my songs in 1975, *'Sweet America'* and *'Free the Lady'*.

She told me that she was playing a concert at the Queen Elizabeth Theatre in a few weeks, and she was hoping that I could come to the theatre and meet her that night. Buffy added that *'Sweet*

America' was an important song, and that she has always wanted to meet the composer.

'*Yes, I would love to meet you, Buffy.*'

She arranged for two tickets to be left at will-call, for me and Macartney, my daughter. Back-stage-laminates would be included. Macartney, was dressed to the nines, wearing her shiny patent leather dress-up shoes, embroidered lace socks, a white pleated skirt, and her favourite blouse, the one with horses on it. She was five. A night on the town for the Greenfields. I was a single parent and loved the honour of raising this special person.

I read about Buffy's 1975 release, '*Sweet America*', in the trades. I purchased a copy. I was excited to hear how she, and Henry Lewy, a well-respected engineer/producer, had interpreted my two '*Blue Sky*' songs. I liked them both. She closely followed my arrangement. It worked well with her distinctive vocal. I loved hearing '*Free the Lady*' interpreted by a feminist. I imagined that most songwriters would have some level of interest in another artist's vision of their song. I certainly do.

Buffy's version of the song '*Sweet America*' was received well in the UK. Her label ABC Records had re-titled her album '*Sweet America*', which was unusual, as Buffy wrote ten of the tracks, and me, only two. To choose my song as the title and banner, was a compliment and an honour. Occasionally, I meet people who are quick to share that they had become aware of my songwriting because of Buffy's version of '*Sweet America*'. That is a wonderful gift.

'*Sweet America*' had good company. Protest music has many outstanding songs in its long history. '*Blowing in the Wind*', '*Galveston*', and '*Masters of War*'. The BBC banned McCartney's '*Give Ireland Back to the Irish*', as was the Boomtown Rats, '*I Don't Like Mondays*'. Radio back in the day, leant towards '*Sugar, Sugar*', ''*Crocodile Rock*'', avoiding political material when able.

I first heard of Buffy when Donovan sang her great protest song '*Universal Soldier*' in 1965. She explained, '*It's about individual responsibility for war and how the old feudal thinking kills us all.*' Buffy thinks like I do, songwriting can be more than a simple '*I love you!*' I wondered if Buffy would sing '*Sweet America*' at the concert that evening.

Arriving at the theatre we donned our beautiful backstage laminates, and then we seamlessly made our way to Buffy. She was waiting for us outside her dressing room wearing a big grin. We went to a private area and talked for forty-five minutes. I asked her, what had made her choose my two songs. Her reply fascinated me.

'Barry, I took my finished album, 'Wynken, Blynken, and Nod' to ABC Records, and they rejected it. Their reason, 'Buffy it must have singles on it. There is not one here'. She continued, ' Henry Lewy, my producer and engineer, came to the rescue'

Henry co-produced and engineered recordings of many critically acclaimed and successful rock and folk albums of the 1970s and 1980s. Joni, *(including 'The Hissing of Summer Lawns', 'Blue', 'Court and Spak')* Leonard Cohen, Neil Young, *('Harvest'),* Judee Sill, Minnie Riperton, and many others.

Buffy continued,

'Henry told me that Joni had mentioned a Canadian songwriter, Barry Greenfield. She thought that his songs were excellent.'

Buffy asked Henry to telephone Joni to discuss these Greenfield compositions. He did. Henry said that Joni thought that both 'Sweet America' and 'Free the Lady' would be a natural fit for me. She sent the LP to Henry to play for Buffy.

Buffy smiled and added,

'I knew instantly that they were right for me, and that they would mesh nicely with the existing ten tracks on 'Wynken, Blynken, and Nod'. 'We got to work, and Henry, the band and I recorded your two songs. ABC Records were ecstatic, re-titled the LP 'Sweet America', and released the title track as the first single'.

I had no idea about any of this, but I was thrilled to know at last how it came to be.

Time was up. Her stage crew advised that she was needed for her vocal warm up. Macartney silent throughout, was given a long hug and told some flattering words by Buffy about herself and her dad. Then Buffy turned to me, pulled me in tight, and whispered in my right ear,

'Barry, one day you will be famous for these two songs.'

She was gone.

We loved the show. She was dressed in a beautiful, soft-leather, light-brown, pant suit, with fringe, that she had worn backstage that night. Buffy sang her catalogue. *'Universal Soldier'* being the high point for me. At *'Sweet America'* she sang my music mentioning me by name. The evening was brilliant. Unforgettable. Her positivity for my songs touched the centre of my heart. Having Macartney share this night was the cherry on the cake.

I drove home watching my five-year-old daughter sleeping in the car. Beautiful. I had an amazing evening. None of it would have happened if I had not driven to the stone house in Half-Moon Bay, to share a gift of my music with one of the great singer songwriters of our time.

I had no expectations that day, I just did what I always have done and continued to do to this day. Share the songs that I write. They are a part of me. No expectations merely positivity in the heart.

Thank you, Ms. Mitchell. Thank You Ms. Sainte-Marie.

Footnote:

'IF'

    1. If I had not driven to Sechelt, to gift 'Blue Sky' to Joni Mitchell.

    2. If the caretaker was not on site, and I did not learn about The Lighthouse pub.

    3. If Joni did not pick up 'Blue Sky' at her mail-drop.

    4. If Joni had never played the LP and loved it.

    5. If ABC Records had not been strict about their non-negotiable need for singles with Buffy, and released 'Wynken, Blynken, and Nod'.

    6. If Henry Lewy did not work for Buffy and Joni.

7. *If Joni had not mentioned to Henry that she liked my songs.*

8. *If Henry would not have thought of suggesting my songs, and then called Joni.*

9. *If Joni had not sent my LP to Henry, who played it for Buffy, who loved it.*

10. *If they had not recorded 'Sweet America' and 'Free the Lady".*

11. *If Buffy's label had not thought my two songs were an improvement for her LP and provided her with the additional budget.*

12. *If ABC Records did not retitle the LP 'Sweet America' and choose it to be the single, it would not have been a success in the UK.*

Two of my songs would not have been heard by so many.

11

An evening with Supertramp at the Queen Elizabeth Theatre, 'Crime of the Century Tour' in 1975

Age 24. I lived alone in a second floor flat in the heart of the Vancouver neighbourhood of Kitsilano. A two-bedroom, with two cats, Rosh, and Masara. It was July 31st, 1975, a lazy Sunday afternoon, summery, nice summery, not too hot. I was relaxing with my gurian six string guitar. TV purring, Manchester United versus Everton at Old Trafford. United two, Everton one. I was drinking Darjeeling tea and munching on the occasional chocolate digestive biscuit. Sunday was always my favourite day, and it still is. I was writing a new song, *'I Carry'*, a song about people I saw, and feared, when visiting America, who were armed with handguns, in restaurants, the mall, everywhere. Concealed or openly carried. They would proudly announce that *'I Carry'*.

> *In his glovebox in his ford*
> *He always carries'*
> *In the store in the bar*
> *In the office in the car*
> *He always carries'*
> *He doesn't feel dressed*
> *Without a handgun In his pocket*
> *He never feels safe in this world*
> *Be prepared, carry*

No one had cell phones back then. We all had attached phones, in the kitchen, or bedroom. Mine rang. I do not like answering phones, but
 I answered.
 "Greenfield? It's Bruce' he barked.
 Life is what happens when you are busy doing nothing.

I knew that gruff, loud bark. Bruce Allan was the '*Big-Boy*' in Vancouver. He was the cock of the walk. He ran Bruce Allen Talent Promotions, where he booked local bands. Making money by sitting in an office, yelling at people on the telephone. The 100, or more, musicians he represented, were on the road, busy working, sleeping in cheap hotel rooms, playing in sweaty bars all over the Province, feeding twenty percent into Bruce Allen Talent Promotions. A fat cat getting fatter. He thought his role, impresario was the important cog-in- the-wheel. Wrong. It's the hard working musician playing 4 hours a night in a smoke filled, beer smelling, rock room, who owns the key to the 18 wheeler. Without some long haired, early twenties, musician, who had practiced hard, for ten gruelling, 10 years, playing Fender Bass *you ain't got a show.* It's the music that matters. Allen drove a Black Corvette convertible with the license plate 'UNRULY'.

Bruce did not phase me. Like most bullies he was transparent. Bruce Allan had signed Bachman Turner Overdrive in 1973, and they took him to another level, internationally. Later he managed Bryan Adams, and Michael Bublé. Bruce knew his stuff. The music business is a good fit for the aggressive, alpha male type, who understands the game, and how to be ruthless and dominant.

I first met Allan in early 1968 when I was 17. He asked me to write three songs for his first band, Five Man Cargo. I always earned his respect. Five Man Cargo used all three of my compositions.

'Barry, do you want to play tonight? Can you open for Supertramp at the Queen Elizabeth Theatre?'

Bruce Allan never needed, or waited, for a reply, he continued,

'Triumvirat, (who were opening for Supertramp), had been busted for illegal drugs in Salt Lake City, and they can't play this evening. They cannot cross the border into Canada'. He had a problem. Fix it and Greenfield is always reliable.

Triumvirat, based in Cologne western Germany, were a key figure in Eurock, a tributary of Progressive Rock coming out of Europe. Their brand was labelled Krautrock. They formed in 1969, and their sound was similar to Emerson Lake and Palmer. Heavy. Power merchants. Loud. This made Greenfield a weird choice to select to open for Supertramp. There were lots of power trios on his books.

'What/huh/Supertramp?' I mumbled back.
'It pays $400. The sound check is at 4pm at the Q.E.'
'OK Bruce, how long a set?'
'45 minutes'.

Bruce Allan talks fast. He uses a minimum number of words, staccato sounding phrases. He wants an answer pronto. He won't accept, *'let me think about it'*.

'OK Bruce, I'll do it. See you at the Q.E. at 4pm. Thank you.'

Like a UFC Martial Artist, one must stay ready, so when the opportunity to fight arrives, you are fit, strong and at the right weight. You must work hard in the gym, daily, stay mentally fit, always. Keep alert, so that when UFC CEO Dana White, or the big dog, Bruce Allan, calls, you are ready, prepared, and you can say *'Yes'*. I constantly practiced my songs, had all the chord changes, and lyrics, compartmentalized. I could do a two-hour gig at the drop of a hat, forty-five minutes, was nothing. I had a few hours notice for that night at Vancouver's Queen Elizabeth Theatre, but I was confident I could open, and bring it, for Supertramp. To date, the biggest concert of my fledgling career.

Me? I am basically your soft-spoken mild-mannered, singer-songwriter. More Clark Kent than Superman. More George Harrison than Keith Richards. I'm not metal. I'm not loud. To this day, the common thinking is Barry is *'Cat-Stevens-like'*. So why did Allan choose me and not one of his power trios?

Bruce picked me because I was reliable. I sing in tune (kind of). I entertain. I had no gear to worry about. Give the kid a stool, a microphone, and he will win the hearts and minds of most who listen. Plus, I was cheap. $400 is much less than a three-piece Krautrock unit from Cologne. In the July 1975 drug-paranoid-world, you did not cross the US/Canadian border carrying illegal substances.

I had less that two hours till soundcheck. Imagine that. Wake up at 8am. No plans. Work on a song, then boom…. the Queen Elizabeth Theatre in two hours!

'Life is what happens, while we are busy drinking Kenyan coffee'.

Arriving at the QE, I was assigned dressing room 'B'. My name was on the door. I put down my extra blue denim work shirt (my stage costume for the night) and followed the signs to backstage. It was empty of people, but full of gear. Supertramp gear. An amazing amount of stuff. Laid out beautifully. I had never been backstage at a prestigious theatre until this moment. I had never worn a laminate. The yellow umbrella that symbolized Supertramp's *'Crime of the Century'* LP, was hanging above Rick Davies Hammond B3 organ, ready for *'School'* the opener. I got chills. I felt apprehension. I was elated to be a part of the festivities.

Supertramp's *'Crime of the Century'* was being promoted, and featured, on this 1975 Canadian Tour. It was their third album, and their first internationally successful one. Especially in the UK, Germany, and Canada. In Canada it went *'Diamond'*. A million sales. I had bought it. It was my favourite non-Beatle solo LP of the time. It was a piece of art. Intense. Brilliant. Smart. I loved *'Rudy'*, *'Dreamer'*, *'Crime'*.

Here I am, about to open the show where *'Crime of the Century'* would be revisited by the artist. In truth, I don't remember being overwhelmed, but I do recall being impressed by the stage layout, the room and the general anticipatory vibe that permeated the environment. To be given an opportunity to share my music with Supertramp's audience, was a big deal for me. I had been to this theatre many times, as an audience member.

I walked slowly out of the wings, and headed to the waiting wooden stool, centre stage. I sat down, picked up my guitar from the stand it was sitting in, and I began to tune. In 1975 one tuned by ear, not by a *'snark'* or *'tuning -peddle'*. Listen to any Neil Young Live LP from that period. Neil tunes by ear before most songs. The Beatles did too. It's a human way to play. I now use both methods.

The Soundman's English accent came through a stage monitor from nowhere. I was already perched on my stool.

'You Barry?'
'Yes'.
'Is that stool and side table, ok for you?'
'yes thanks'.

I gazed out at 3000 empty seats. Gulped. Fear set in. What have I agreed too? Here I was in the big time. A giant leap for me.

The sound check went well. The soundman was professional, and appreciative. Three, maybe four songs. *'Rodeo', Concert Fever'* I recall were the first two. One up and bright, the second gentle with plectrum picked individual strings, just as it was written in Thunder Bay on the John Lee Hooker tour in 1972.

'You sound great Barry, but I need one more please'.

I decided to play a song that was not in that night's repertoire. In fact, I had never sung it to anyone, anywhere. It was not one of mine. It was a new experience to hear *'me'* that good and clear, so I decided to play something for me to hear. A song I played alone on my couch. My arrangement of Paul's and John's *'She Loves You'*. It was a perfect Beatle song, and I wanted to share this important day with The Lads somehow. So, I bit down on the bit and delivered a 1963 Liverpool classic.

I was 12 when I first heard this single. Nothing has ever sounded that alive, it captured the element of fun, it was new, exhilarating. *'She Loves You'*, was recorded in a maelstrom at EMI Studios. Pandemonium, with girl fans running wild and free through the halls of EMI, after breaking into the building. The Lads loved the excitement.

Paul and John started composing *'She Loves You'* on 26 June 1963 after a concert in Newcastle, on the Roy Orbison tour. It was born on the tour bus and continued later that night at their hotel in Newcastle. Paul recalls,

'we sat in the hotel bedroom for a few hours and wrote it – John and I, sitting on twin beds with guitars'.(1)

This idea of the song was attributed by John to his partner Paul, in 1980. John addressed the songs genesis,

'It was Paul's idea, instead of singing 'I love you' again, we'd have a third party. That kind of little detail is still in his work. He will write a story about someone. I'm more inclined to write about myself'. (2)

The Soundman's voice appeared for a last time. *'Great. See you tonight. You sound wonderful Barry. Thanks, for joining us with such little notice mate.''*

I remained like a crow perched on the stool, drinking the view, smiling inside, and loving this day…...when………..

'Hello. I wanted to say thank you for helping us out.'

It was Rodger Hodgson, my favourite member of Supertramp. He was a guitarist extraordinaire, superb singer, the glorious composer of *'The Logical Song', 'Dreamer'*. A huge talent, from the great UK town of Portsmouth.

'Thank you, for this splendid opportunity', I stuttered back at him.

'Who arranged the Beatle song?' he asked me.

'I did!'

I had no idea that Rodger Hodgson had been in the wings. I did not know how long he had been watching me. But he had witnessed me singing, *'She Loves You'*. Looking directly at me he said, *'Barry it's bloody brilliant'*.

'Thank you very much'.

I told Rodger that I thought that no one pays attention to the superb lyric that John and Paul wrote in '63. All that people hear is *'Yeah, yeah, yeah'* He thought about it, and agreed.

> *You know it's up to you*
> *I think it's only fair*
> *Pride can hurt you, too*
> *Apologize to her*
> *Because she loves you*
> *And you know that can't be bad*
> *Yes, she loves you*
> *And you know you should be glad,*
> *She loves you*

'Do you have time to talk?', he asked.

'Love to'.

We sat backstage on two comfortable easy chairs, perhaps from a stage set. We shared an hour talking music; our love for The Beatles; the craft of song writing, Canada, about favourite records. Dreams. He was a spiritual guy; we had a connection. We were the same age. I have always found immense joy on the highway to art, it is a gift that keeps on giving. He, like me, was focused on music not commerce. Music heals.

Supertramp were formed in London in 1970. Rodger Hodgson, Rick Davies (writer, piano), Dougie Thomson (bass), Bob Siebenberg (kit), and John Helliwell (MC and sax). Sixty million LPs sold. As good a band as any, anywhere, anytime. Tight. Brilliant. Their music is still a joy even now. They hit a rich vein with *'Crime'*, *'Quietest Moments'* *'Crisis what Crisis'*, and *'Breakfast in America'*.

Looking at their *'Crime of the Century'* stage set I was at once scared, and yet comfortable. I sensed that Rodger, like me, sought humanity that can be found in the world of music, every night that he performed, not just another box ticked off, another paycheque. A kindred spirit. I belonged there. I had arrived. I was so excited to play with Supertramp.

8pm……the lights came down. A deep voiced DJ from some local FM station, walked out into the centre stage spotlight. Revealing a single stool, my side table, two microphones, (my guitar was miked in 1975), and my gurian in its stand.

'Good evening music lovers. I have some sad news. Triumvirat won't be playing tonight. The band was unable to cross the border into Canada. Refunds are available at the box office for any who want it………. but we have in their place, Vancouver's own, Barry Greenfield'.

He ran off. I remember that. He actually ran!

I walked on, smiling.

The boos grew louder with each step I took. Some clapped. Some got up, and left their seats, heading for the door. I hadn't played a note. They would rather have a drink in the Queen Elizabeth bar than share the night with a long haired, folk singer. I estimate that thirty percent of a full room walked out. I was horrified and became very unsettled and fearful. Booing has that effect on me. I sat down and smiled again.

'Thanks for coming. Boy am I happy to be here tonight. I am going to sing songs I have written and share a few true stories. Let's make the most of this special night. Supertramp are excited to perform for you'.

I opened my set with *'Rodeo'*, *'………'I broke my heart sometime ago, so I joined this rodeo, to try to earn myself some fame....'* An upbeat Barry song that I generally opened my night with. The next 45 minutes flew by. I did a good, cohesive, thoughtful set. Sang strong, made them laugh, and as I looked out into the QE, I kept seeing more and more people walking back into the room, they wanted to hear, and see, why the audience was clapping loudly, occasionally whooping, and appreciating the guy on the stool. I earned a double encore. *'Free the Lady'* and *'New York Is Closed Tonight'*. My song that many knew from months of airplay on the radio. It was the most played song on Canadian airways a few years earlier.

Playing at the Queen Elizabeth Theatre, the premiere performing arts venue in Vancouver, was spectacular. I love *soft seaters*. To this day that's my optimum venue. Nearly 3000 soft seats, sloping uphill, great sight lines from both levels, orchestra and mezzanine, and precise sound. The stage was huge. Daunting. When I walked out for the sound check, and again at 8pm for my set, it felt like an aircraft hangar. The theatre has a 70' wide x 40' deep stage/performing area.

Entering to loud booing from the Triumvirat fans was unsettling. Yet, one must know sadness to understand joy. I accepted it, and I understood it. Surely a sign saying 'no Triumvirat tonight', at the theatre entrance, would have been a better way to handle it. I guess the promoter, Bruce Allan, wanted the buying public inside the room, cozy and settled, ready to go, when the bomb was dropped. I have no idea how many asked for a refund, but the theatre appeared full. I assume it was minimal. The businesspeople pocketed the profit they sought.

The sight of the crowd slipping back into the theatre to witness the folky guy was surprising and extremely satisfying. It began as a trickle, but by mid show it was obvious that word had reached the foyer. I remember the sweet feeling of relief, and an overwhelming state of joy that covered me on my set's completion. 'New York is Closed Tonight' received a semi-standing ovation. Beautiful. Memorable for this songwriter.

A man I have never met, but I have had correspondence with whilst researching *'My Journey to Blue Sky'*, was at the Theatre that night in 1975. Leonard Albert (Bert) Goulet. He lives in Dawson Creek, BC. He was 18 and in the audience when the DJ announced me. He wrote this about his memory of that concert.

'Back in the day Supertramp came to the QE with a backup band called Triumvirat, an ELP style band which all of us Proggers were looking forward to seeing but they had to cancel. Lots of rumbling in the foyer about it and who was going to replace them. This guy, Barry Greenfield, walked out and was super soothing,

which looking back probably was a good thing, because it flowed so sweetly into the Supertramp vibe'.

After my hour in the spotlight, I found myself alone in dressing room 'B'. I reflected silently. I changed into a dry, clean shirt. Put my guitar away, after cleaning it with a cloth. Drank more water.

The helter skelter way the day went didn't allow me to bring a friend to share the night. My sister, Suzan, would have loved to have attended, but I was so focused on my preparation that I didn't even consider the logistics of guests. It was destined to be an experience for a solitary man.

The hallways backstage were well marked and after one Spinal Tap bad decision, I found the wings. Supertramp were standing there, waiting to walk on. Rodger leaned into me, and said,

'Beautiful set Barry'.

He had watched. I mentioned something like *'break a leg Rodger'*, and then I slipped into the shadows, not wishing to intrude. Then it became magical, Rick Davies was playing the harmonica intro into *'School'*. The audience went wild. Then like Apollo 11 they took off. The set was 90 minutes of mostly *'Crime'*. Some songs I didn't know, but most I did. Roger shone like a diamond. Helliwell talked too much but played great clarinet. Rick held his own. Dougie Thomson on bass, the only American, Bob Siebenberg on drums were locked in. Perfect. The set was immaculate. Record identical. Flawless in delivery. Bigger and better live. A night to remember.

I went home on the bus alone. Thinking about Rodger and his kind words. I still play Supertramp frequently on my home system. *'Breakfast in America'* (1979) and *'Crime of the Century'* (1974) are most the most special.

My night opening slot for Supertramp certainly was that….special.

Footnote:

I took many lessons away from that night.

If a door opens walk through it, if it feels right, it is right.

Face your fears, don't deny them.

Always be ready. Always have good strings on your guitar, and a clean shirt in the closet.

Be positive as you walk through life. Be grateful for what comes your way.

Make a stranger feel like a friend.

If they boo the cheers sound louder and go straight to the heart.

The biggest take away was, when performing, smile, especially if they boo.

This only occurred once in my career, on July 31, 1975, when I opened for Supertramp.

12

The Art of Song Writing – My passion

Many amazing souls excel in their chosen vocation. Their choices, their habits and methods are an excellent guide, and a teaching source for the beginner. If the student studies these traits and behaviours, they can incorporate the ones that fit into their regime and improve. This is true for artists, track and field competitors, scholars, archaeologists, military planners et.al. One can glean a great deal by reading biographies, watching interviews and studying the leaders in their chosen field. How do you get to Carnegie Hall, practice.

Great golfers are consumed with golf, frequently from an early age. Tiger Woods was up at 4am for two hours each day to practice one aspect of his game. This was repeated after school, same golf element, two hours. Putting, driving, sand traps. The same is true for an ATP ranked tennis player. They start swinging a junior racket when young. Serving, volleying, back hand. A Kentucky Derby jockey, an Apollo astronaut, even a great Russian Chess Grandmaster, start to research their chosen paths in their youth. Perfecting by practicing. They develop an everlasting love for their chosen field. A passion that fills their cup to the brim. Joseph Kosuth, a leader of conceptual art, Paul McCartney, working with James, his father on piano styles, Sally Ride, NASA, were students of the successful.

I began my romance with songwriting in 1956. Age five. I had a deep feeling, a strong pull, towards music. The introduction came via an English singer, Frankie Vaughan, who sang a blues based tune '*The Green Door.*' Vaughan sang:

An old piano that was playing hot
Behind the green door
Don't know what they're doing

> *But they laugh a lot*
> *Behind the green door*

The words pulled me into a new world, a world that existed only behind the green door. A world of intrigue and danger. The unknown lurked in the shadows behind the door that was green. I wanted to knock, open, walk through that door and enter that world.

Another root on the musical tree was Vic Damone, a crooner, who sang, *'On the Street Where You Live'*. Damone was poetic, and like so many from this period they sang words that were soothing to the ear and the heart. Nat King Cole, Sinatra, Dean Martin, Ella Fitzgerald, and Joe Williams come to mind.

> *I have often walked down the street before*
> *But the pavement always stayed beneath my feet before.*
> *Are there lilac trees*
> *In the heart of town?*
> *Can you hear a lark in any other part of town?*
> *Does enchantment pour out of every door?*
> *No, it's just on the street where you live.*

These were charming, memorable words. Poetry, beautifully composed by Alan Jay Lerner and Frederick Loewe. Each phrase familiar and explanatory about the neighborhood where she lived. An amazing lyric. Paul McCartney did the same with *'Eleanor Rigby'* decades later. *'Suzanne'* by Leonard Cohen a third example of lyrics as a painting. *'River'* written by Joni Mitchell a fourth.

I was a pre-teen when I became inspired by Frankie Laine who sang *'Ghost Riders in the Sky'*. Laine told me a story:

> *'Yippie aye yay, yippie aye oh'*
> *An old cowpoke who rode out, one dark and windy day*
> *When all at once a mighty herd*
> *Of red eyed cows he saw*
> *Plowin' through the ragged skies*
> *And up the cloudy draw*
> *'Yippie aye yay, yippie aye oh'*

That mesmerized me. A song about *'Ghost Riders'*. Marvelous! A cowboy to a Mancunian was a fantasy character. Roy Rogers, Hopalong Cassidy, The Lone Ranger, were black and white fictional, fantasy characters to an English boy living in the box room, in a semi detached, on Kendall Road, in Cheetham Hill. Frankie Laine introduced ghost riders to me with words that painted a vivid picture for the kid.

These three early songs provided me with a blueprint, a treasure map, that I could follow. Gold waited at the end of the rainbow, on the sunny side of the street, on the spot marked X. I found songs that spoke to me. Songs that I thought were different. Songs who's aim, I believed, was true. Songs that were written with thought and inspiration. Elvis's *'Wooden Heart', 'Volare (Nel blu dipinto di blu)' sung by Domenico Modugno, and the wonderful 'All I Have to Do Is Dream' by the silky Everly Brothers.*

The choice in front of me was to choose and pursue the path of the melody writer or the avenue of the lyricist. As I was not naturally gifted musically, my lure was the words. *'How Much is that Doggie in the Window, the one with the waggly tail'*, a classic written by Bob Merrill and performed by Patti Page, it seemed so original and clever to my young ears. Or the classic song covered by so many, '*(You give me) Fever', written* by Eddie Cooley and Otis Blackwell. Hot and dangerous, its tone made it stand out. Peggy Lee's attitude was the new, ruthless aggression.

My introduction to the brilliant early music of Elvis Presly was a song written by Wally Gold, Aaron Schroeder and Eduardo di Capua, *'Now or Never'*. A beautiful lyric sung by the man with the perfect voice. A knockout of a record and a complete song. It is always important to keep the words in line with the title. Do not stray. Keep it focused and in the box. *'Now or Never'*, is all that and more.

'It's now or never, come hold me tight, kiss me my darling, be mine tonight. Tomorrow will be too late, it's now or never, my love won't wait, it's now or never.'

I committed these songs to memory and sang them repeatedly. I had begun studying songs. Ears close to the radio speaker in our front room. Looking for the nuggets hiding in the stones, seeking out berries sleeping inside the weeds. I was exhilarated when I discovered a gem. I was about to get a jolt, an overload of brilliance in 1963, The Beatles.

At first it was the early singles, *'Please Please Me'*, *'From Me to You'*, *'She Loves You'* and *'I Want to Hold Your Hand'*. I heard them over and over on my radio. They were fresh, tight, happy, joyous and new. Then a seismic change occurred. The world went from black and white to technicolour. In November 1963, The Beatles released their second LP, *'With the Beatles'*.

I studied, *'It Won't Be Long'* by John Lennon, *'Don't Bother Me'*, by George Harrison and *'All My Loving'* by Paul McCartney. Doors and windows flew open. The vista that I witnessed was transformative. I still feel goosebumps when I play that LP. 'With The Beatles' cemented Beatlemania, because each song was magical. Their entire catalogue was joyful, and this helped me stay positive, be excited, and want to write. This 1963 LP is filled with magnificent original material. I sensed that *'there was gold in them there hills'*. It was as fresh as the first snow, as exciting as when I first saw Victoria Falls, or the afternoon I kissed my wife Lori, for the first time, at Spanish Banks.

Many bands write songs and fill their mundane, eponymous LPs with them.
　Yes, the lines rhyme, ABACAB, the melody is too often unoriginal, borrowed and predictable. They use a well-worn traditional chord pattern, C A minor F G. Sure, they may have written a song, a song that lists them as the composer on the record sleeve, but they are not songwriters, they have simply written a song. There is a difference. Picasso was a painter, so is my mother-in-law. Same descriptive noun, but Lori's mom is no-Picasso.
　Burt Bacharach, Elton John, Björn Ulvaeus, Benny Andersson, Prince, Sheryl Crow, Kris Kristoffersen, George Harrison, Joni Mitchell, Bob Dylan, Stevie Wonder, Jimmy Webb, Andrew Lloyd Webber, Paul McCartney, Leonard Cohen, Kate Bush, and others are songwriters. Mentors all.
My first steps in attempting to become a songwriter arrived at fourteen. I used an unusual entry point; I found song titles that intrigued me.

The Daily News in Durban, South Africa, printed the UK top ten. I would walk to the newsagent and buy the Saturday newspaper. Then I would read the ten song titles on the British Hit Parade. I would pick one, and write my own tune, using the title that I read, as my starting point. Yes, truth is stranger than fiction.

Two early titles that I selected for this process were *'You Can't Do That'* by John Lennon, and Pete Townsend's, *'My Generation'*. I used these two titles as a springboard to create an original lyric, and then a Greenfield melody. The idea was to compose a three-minute original Greenfield song using a mentor's hit title. This became my routine for a year. I wrote my first 10 songs using this method. It worked.

I had never heard The Beatles version of *'You Can't Do That'*, or The Who sing *'My Generation'* till much later. The South African Apartheid Regime fed us radio with its menu built on a steady diet of Jim Reeves, Rosemary Clooney and Eddy Arnold. Easy listening music like Mantovani, a light orchestral style entertainer, and The Andrew Sisters, three safe American white ladies. No music of colour, or music that borrowed from that genre.

My words imagined from the title 'You Can't Do That' were:

Listen to me stop and wait
You can't do that baby
It will make us late
If you do I'll close the gate
You can't do that

My words imagined from the title 'My Generation' were:

My generation have fun at school
My generation don't follow rules, no no no
Not my generation
We are young and strong
We play all day long
My generation

I did not have a songwriting teacher; I did not own a songwriting book. I simply did it. I invented songs. After a year I composed my first original song, *'Josephine'*. Not a real person, a fictitious tune. I selected a name that I thought made an unusual title. A song title must be strong such as, *'A Well-Respected Man'*, written by Ray Davies; *'Blowin' in the Wind'*, written by Bob Dylan; and *'Here Comes the Night'* written by Bert Berns.

My words for *'Josephine'* were:

> *Many years you were my girl Josephine*
> *Then you weren't my only pearl Josephine*
> *Now that you're gone*
> *You've gained my esteem*
> *Josephine*

I remember the melody, and the simple chord structure of my first attempt at writing a full song, *'Josephine'*. The chords used were:

G CD GA MinorD Grepeat.

The lyrics were charming, childlike.

I kept going where my heart led me. If you do something with passion, and care, you improve. My Hilroy 40 pages school exercise books, nine inches by seven inches, quickly filled. I wrote *'Barry's Songs'* on the covers of each notebook. Volumes One, Two, Three. Paul McCartney and John Lennon also wrote their lyrics on scraps of paper, and schoolbooks. They said that if you could not remember the melody, then it probably was not strong enough. That was the philosophy I adopted.

I played all *'the new ones'* to my sister and my mother. Naturally, they were biased, they loved them all. However, I did pay attention, and I remembered their favourites. I improved rapidly.

At age 17 I felt ready to leave the comfort of the family audience. I hitch-hiked to Los Angeles from Vancouver in 1968. My intent was to find out if strangers, who worked in the music business, saw value in my art. It took me three long days, and three endless nights to travel the thirteen hundred miles. The worst night was the night I slept in my sleeping bag in an abandoned gas station in Northern California. I saw a snake. I was terrified. In the City of Angels, I stayed in a B-Movie, seedy, motel on Sunset Boulevard, I think it was called 'Come On Inn'.

I visited a dozen music business offices in the three days that I spent in smoggy, busy, LA. I used the Yellow Pages to select offices. Walking to office buildings that were miles away. Sometimes, I got 30 minutes of their attention, in others less. A few of the offices, I did not get past the receptionist. The ones that listened gave a similar response, some more kindly than others.

'Good stuff, Barry. I don't hear anything golden in these songs but keep at it'.

It gave me a sense of accomplishment. I saw it as a successful trip. I grew in knowledge and listened to all that gave me the time. I rode the Greyhound bus back to Canada. A full 24 hours, a lot of it I was feeling a bit bus sick.

To this day when I finish *'a new song'*, I always learn more about who I am. It provides me with some life understanding and clarity. I like to write about varied subjects. Be it about Lori, *('I Love that Woman')*, my daughter, (*'Barleycorn'*), a topical subject, like pollution (*'New York is Closed Tonight'*), a thoughtful look at our planet ('Water is the New Gold'), or a life lesson, ('Carjacked Ford').

The most common question a songwriter gets is,
'What comes first, the words or the music?'

My answer is the same answer that I have read or heard, given by many songwriters. Every permutation possible occurs. There is no pre-thought to my songwriting. I never think about writing a love song, or a political song, or a bluesy tune. I just listen to the heart and try to understand what it is telling me to express. Sometimes I see, or occasionally, I think of a phrase that speaks to me. Two examples that come to mind are *'Bamboo Sheets'* (2016) and *'Invisible Baggage'* (2024). At times, when I am playing, a chord patten grabs my attention, a jumping off point. Other times I may be jamming, and something happens, I simply follow it. Many roads up any mountain will lead you to the summit.

The story of '*I'm Not in Love*' which I heard from the source, Stewart and Gouldman, speaks volumes to that fact. '*I'm Not in Love*' has enjoyed lasting popularity, with over three million plays on US radio since its release. It won three Ivor Novello Awards in 1976 for Best Pop Song, International Hit of the Year, and Most Performed British Work. An accomplished song.

Eric came up with the idea for '*I'm Not in Love*'. He wanted to speak honestly to his wife about his love for her, via a song, but he decided to use an unusual route, a unique lyrical approach. He decided to deliver it from a less predictable angle. Eric explained that he wanted to write a song whose words said,

'I'm not in love with you', while subtly giving all the reasons throughout the song why I could never let go of this relationship'.

Eric wrote most of the melody, and all the lyrics, before taking it to the studio to show it to Graham, who offered to help him complete the song. Graham wrote improved chords for part of the melody, and added the simple, but memorable, intro, Aadd2/B Badd2/B G#m7, and bridge,

'*ooo you'll wait a long time for me'.*

Graham told me that he and Eric spent three days perfecting this giant. Then the duo took their work to the other duo in 10cc, Lol and Kevin. The rest is history. A song that changed the musical world for so many, me included. Graham played me the original idea for the song's tempo in his kitchen, it had a bossa nova feel. It sounded wonderful but was soon dropped by all four in their initial discussions.

So many songs have wonderful birthing stories. Another historic song that shaped so many songwriters was John Lennon's 1966 opus, '*Strawberry Field's Forever*'.

Strawberry Fields was the name of a childhood haunt frequented by a young Lennon and his Quarry Bank High School mates. It was a Salvation Army children's home close to John's home, in Woolton, Liverpool. (1)

John's aunt Mimi recalled:

'There was something about the place that always fascinated John. He could see it from his window ... He used to hear the Salvation Army band [playing at the garden party], and he would pull me along, saying, 'Hurry up, Mimi – we're going to be late.' (2)

The song was composed by John during the filming of *'How I Won the War'* John's first, and only, solo acting role. It was filmed in Spain. *'John was feeling vulnerable, without his Beatle mates,'* according to his wife, Cynthia. (3). His first separation from the Band. They had been *'living in a suitcase'* since Hamburg. The Beatles worked most days, every year. Always together, taking on the world as a unit, the *'four headed monster'*, Keith Richards dubbed them. Being alone was a touch scary for this sensitive artist, John, who never liked to appear vulnerable.

In the first versions that Lennon committed to tape, in September, there was no reference to Strawberry Field. Author Steve Turner says that at this stage, Lennon most likely drew inspiration from Nikos Kazantzakis's autobiographical novel *Report to Greco*, which he was reading in Almería and "*tells of a writer searching for spiritual meaning". (*4)

John wrote songs at two speeds. Full-speed ahead, where songs were created in a few hours, and slow-speed, over weeks, sometimes months. Without Paul sitting across from him, eye to eye, acoustic to acoustic, John began to see his songs as a vehicle through which he could talk about himself. *'Help'*, *'Nowhere Man'*, *'In My Life'*.

For the chorus, Lennon was once again inspired by childhood memories in his use of the phrase, *'nothing to get hung about'* were inspired by Aunt Mimi's strict order not to play in the grounds of Strawberry Field, to which Lennon replied, *'They can't hang you for it'*.(5)

The final destination for *'Strawberry Field's Forever'* took months of diligent, thoughtful input, and hours of hard work, from the Beatles and their extraordinary producer, George Martin, to arrive at. Multi rewrites, many instruments used, some discarded and some kept. Many edits and the use of Veri-speed to get the results required. Finally, a blend of two different takes. *'Strawberry Field's Forever'* went through numerous incantations. When completed the song took its place in musical history, although John derided it in 1980 just prior to his assassination, suggesting Paul sabotaged the recordings. Wow!

Another gift that *'Strawberry Field's Forever'* gave to the Beatle fans, was the fact that it motivated Paul McCartney's glorious composition *'Penny Lane'*. Paul's bookend song to John's masterpiece. Both convey nostalgia for their early years in Liverpool. Both refer to real locations. Paul wrote *'Penny Lane'* after being deeply inspired and moved by John's anthem.

Upon the release of *'Strawberry Fields Forever'*, Pete Townsend described it as *'utterly bizarre, creative, strange and different'*. (6) Mark Lindsay lead vocalist of the American pop giants Paul Revere and The Raiders listened to the single at home with his producer, *'as the song ended, we both just looked at each other. I said, now what are we going to do? With that single, the Beatles raised the ante as to what a pop record should be'*. (7) In another famous anecdote, Brian Wilson, the Beach Boy genius, first heard "*Strawberry Fields Forever*" on his car radio (8) while under the influence of barbiturates (9). Brian said to his passenger Michael Vosse

'They did it already – what I wanted to do with Smile. Maybe it's too late.'

Michael Vosse recalled that they then exchanged laughter, although *'at the moment he (Brian) said it, he sounded very serious'*. (10)

Among these laudatory appraisals, (11). Time magazine hailed the song as "*the latest sample of the Beatles' astonishing inventiveness*". (12).

The Time writer said that:

'Since 1963 The Beatles have developed into the single most creative force in pop music. Wherever they go, the pack follows. And where they have gone in recent months, not even their most ardent supporters would ever have dreamed of. They have bridged the heretofore impassable gap between rock and classical, mixing elements of Bach, Oriental, and electronic music with vintage twang to achieve the most compellingly original sounds ever heard in pop music. (13)

Yes, I have learnt in my studying the art, that it is all about the songwriting.

It all starts with the song, it continues with the song, and it ends with the song. You can have a great voice, play drums superbly, have a beautiful set of harmonies, you can even have nice hair, but without the lyric and the melody you have nothing that will resonate, last, or touch the heart, and reach the soul. You always need a good song. Kate Bush's *'The Kick Inside'*,

> I'm giving it all in a moment or two
> I'm giving it all in a moment for you
> I'm giving it all, giving it, giving it, giving it
> This kicking here inside makes me leave you behind
> No more under the quilt to keep you warm

'Comfortably Numb' by Roger Waters and David Gilmour,

> There is no pain, you are receding
> A distant ship smoke on the horizon
> You are only coming through in waves
> Your lips move but I can't hear what you're saying
> When I was a child I had a fever
> My hands felt just like two balloons
> Now I've got that feeling once again
> I can't explain, you would not understand
> This is not how I am
> I have become comfortably numb

Other examples are Christopher Cross with *'Sailing'*. The Doobie Brothers sang about *'China Grove'*. Joni Mitchell wrote, *'Big Yellow Taxi"*. Neil Diamond delivered *'Sweet Caroline'*. The proof is in the pudding.

Some songwriters specialize in being the lyricist. Others melody. I attempt both.

I have had the pleasure of collaborating with many gifted, and experienced song writers. A nerve-racking endeavour each time. A similar nervousness that I felt when on a date as a teen. But once you clear the first hurdle it becomes a joyous exchange.

Some of my favourite, collaborations, were David Sancious, a member of the E Street Band. We wrote in Woodstock, New York, *('Summerville')*; Chris Nole, John Denver's pianist, in Brentwood, Tennessee, *('The Simple Life')*; Graham Gouldman of 10cc in Hampsted Heath in London, *('Kong Kong')'*; Mick Dalla-Vee, The Wizard Brothers via computer during COVID-19, (*'The Beautiful Band'*); Randy Bachman, BTO, *('It Should Have Been Me')*; Robert Ellis Orral, in Nashville *('The Road Home')*; and my wife Lori Greenfield, in our living room, *('If You Loved Me Again')*. I seldom refuse when offered. Some are famous, household names, others unknown. I have learnt so much from so many.

The music business that I entered in 1967 is different now. But one thread that remained constant, is that it has always involves *'suits'*. People who think about commerce and are not concerned with the art of music. In 1967 I wrote:

> *Don't forget it's the music business*
> *Don't forget where the emphasis is*
> *It used to be the music*
> *Now it's completely on the business*

I had no conception of how much truer these words would become with each passing decade.

One afternoon Lori and I sat in an empty Pho café in Cambie Village. The music was relentless on the restaurant sound system. Dance oriented. We speculated that it was all A I. The instruments, the multi-vocalists, the disappointing tune, all computers. We've retreated a long way from 1969's *'Hey Jude'*, with its soulful piano, great vocals, smooth arrangement, heartfelt lyrics, and freedom of flow.

Before 1962 the songs generally came from writers not from the artists. The songs sung were written by a songwriter, and then sung by the singer.

Examples: Cole Porter, *'Night and Day'*, sung by Fred Astaire, in 1932. Sammy Cahn, *'Three Coins in a Fountain'*, sung beautifully by Frank Sinatra, in 1955. Abel Meeropol composed *'Strange Fruit'* for Billie Holiday in 1939.

These greatly respected songwriters, and wonderful vocalists, shaped my thinking, and helped me understand the art of the process. The arrival of Lennon and McCartney, Paul Simon, Joni Mitchell, Neil Diamond, and later Elton John and Bernie Taupin, opened the flood gates. Their success resulted in every musician and every wannabee with an ego, figuring,

'hey, I can write songs and get rich!'

If only it were that easy!

The golden age of songwriting lasted two decades, but then faded like a candle in the rain. Bob Dylan, Carole King, Leonard Cohen, Pink Floyd, The Stones, were replaced by writers who were motivated by the incentive of air-play royalties, resulting in the standards dropping like a pebble racing to the road when dropped from the roof, gravity.

To explain other perspectives about the forgotten art, I give you the views of four songwriters:

* Neil Young,
'I don't force it. If you don't have an idea and you don't hear anything going over and over in your head, don't sit down and try to write a song. You know, go mow the lawn. My songs speak for themselves'.

* Bob Dylan,
'It is only natural to pattern yourself after someone. But you can't just copy someone. If you like someone's work, the important thing is to be exposed to everything that person has been exposed to'.

* Carole King,
'One of the things that I try to be conscious about in crafting a song is the concept of bringing it home. I like to bring it somewhere familiar, someplace that people feel it's resolved, it's settled'.

* Paul Simon,
'It's very helpful to start with something that's true. If you start with something that's false, you're always covering your tracks. Something simple and true, that has a lot of possibilities, is a nice way to begin."

My most successful penned song is '*New York is Closed Tonight.*' It sat at number one in Canada for weeks. It was written in 30 minutes, on a Sunday afternoon. I was sitting on my couch, flipping through the pages of a glossy magazine, when I found an advertisement for General Electric. Its purpose was to explain that energy needed to be conserved. To enforce their point, they used the picture of a large light bulb burning brightly. It was the only image on the page. Beneath it was the phrase,

'New York is Closed Tonight.'

Always seeking a good, strong, precise title, I knew I had found a candidate. Soon I had thirteen verses. No chorus. No bridge. The thirteen verses were linked by the phrase *'New York is Closed Tonight',* which ended each verse. A Dylan technique, as employed in 'The Gates of Eden',

> *With a time-rusted compass blade*
> *Aladdin and his lamp*
> *Sits with Utopian hermit monks*
> *Side saddle on the Golden Calf*
> *And on their promises of paradise*
> *You will not hear a laugh*
> *All except inside the Gates of Eden*

For my song, *'New York is Closed Tonight,'* I picked the best three verses, and let the other ten float out to sea, forever lost. I kept the cream.

Here is the finished lyric to *'New York Is Closed Tonight'*:

> *My eyes are hurting badly*
> *I'm breathing through my nose*
> *My white shirt is turning gray*
> *I should wear plastic clothes*
> *It's getting dark so early*
> *So long before its night*
> *And the neon freeway sign*
> *Said New York Is Closed Tonight*
> *Breathing's getting harder*
> *As I walk through the park*
>
> *The trees are brown and dingy*
> *And no one walks the dog*
> *My dog died Thursday*
> *I couldn't sleep all night*
> *And the man on the radio*

> *He said New York Is Closed Tonight*
> *Call back your armies*
> *The demonstrations through*
> *Everything is lost*
> *There's nothing we can do*
> *We told you long ago*
> *Your solution was not right*
> *And today the Pittsburgh Herald read*
> *New York Is Closed Tonight*

In 1972, my song won the Harold Moon SOCAN Award, which is the number one award for songwriting in Canada. It was the most played song on Canadian radio that year.

Then 29 years later, on 9/11 nineteen terrorists hijacked four commercial airliners, and crashed the first two planes into the Twin Towers of the World Trade Centre, in New York City. It was the deadliest terrorist attack in history, resulting in closing the City that night, September 11, 2001, New York was closed. All events were cancelled. Landmarks were closed, primarily because of fears that they may be attacked. The entire airspaces of the United States and Canada were closed ("ground stop") by order of FAA National Operations Manager Ben Sliney (who was working his first day in that position) except for military, police, and medical flights. The US stock market was closed for four days. After the attacks my song, *'New York is Closed Tonight,'* was interpreted by some to be about the tragedy. The universe unfolds as it will, and CNN featured it as the musical bed behind video's played on air of the Towers collapsing. Ash covered Manhattan and its residents.

I have written for six decades. I have recorded eleven LP's, all with Greenfield penned music. I am continually surprised when a new one arrives, out-of-the-blue. Herein lies the joy, the mystery and the magic that I have received by being a songwriter.

This book is my story. My journey to Blue Sky.

Barry Greenfield 2024.

Footnote:

- Barry Greenfield

Great songwriters are as rare as great rock climbers. They are born with something. She/he/they can write songs that will make people think, feel, smile, cry, grow angry, laugh, have sex, and fall in love.

- Joni Mitchell

I heard someone from the music business saying they are no longer looking for talent, they want people with a certain look and a willingness to cooperate.

- Graham Nash

I'm trying to communicate here. I'm a communicator, I like to communicate, and if a million people buy it then we've touched a million people, if only ten people buy it, then we've only touched ten, and that's important, because I'm satisfied with only ten. But I love a million.

- Billy Joel

I think music in itself is healing. It's an explosive expression of humanity. It's something we are all touched by. No matter what culture we're from, everyone loves music.

References
1. MacDonald 2005, p. 216.
2. Spitz 2005, p. 642.
3. Turner 2016, pp. 504–05, 537–38
4. Turner 2016, pp. 506–07.
5. "Strawberry Fields is not forever" **Freeman, Simon (31 May 2005).**
6. "From Sgt Pepper to Syd Barrett' **Blake, Mark (19 June 2016).**
7. Babiuk 2002, p. 201.**Babiuk, Andy (2002).** *Beatles Gear: All the Fab Four's Instruments, from Stage to Studio.*

8. Rodriguez 2012, pp. 187–88.
9. *Beautiful Dreamer: Brian Wilson and the Story of Smile* Leaf, David (director) (2004).
10. *"Lost and Found Sounds (page 2)"*. *The Baltimore Sun* Kiehl, Stephen (26 September 2004).
11. Gendron 2002, p. 194.
12. *Time staff (3 March 1967) p. 63.*
13. Spitz 2005, p. 657.
14. *Beautiful Dreamer: Brian Wilson and the Story of Smile* Leaf, David (director) (2004).
15. *"Lost and Found Sounds (page 2)"*. *The Baltimore Sun* Kiehl, Stephen (26 September 2004).
16. Gendron 2002, p. 194.
17. *Time staff (3 March 1967) p. 63.*
18. Spitz 2005, p. 657.

13

The 12 Bar Club, London. 19 September 2006

I have always loved playing my songs live. Set times range from an hour to double that. I only accept gigs, concerts, performance, where the audience listen. It's about the lyrics. I will not play in bars, restaurants, state fairs etc.

I began at age 16, second on the bill, in a small ice rink. I had a three year regular slot opening at Vancouver's fabulous The Egress. An intimate music room that one could find in most Cities in the seventies. I set the plate for the SNL comedian Steve Martin, banjo picker , the 'Gentle on my Mind', songwriter, John Hartford, jazz pianist, Mose Allison, and blues legends, Sonny Terry & Brownie McGhee and countless others.

I fondly remember my sixty minutes with Van Morrison in 1985, in a full 10,000 seat arena. Touring Canada with Cheech and Chong had its uniqueness. I adored Tommy Chong, a true professional. So many shows, so many pairings. Rod Stewart and The Faces, Maria Muldaur, the Murray (no fun) McLaughlin Tour, and so many more.

A staple to my road trips was that I expected to be paid fairly, which would need to provide me a cushion for hotel, travel and per diem. I have played in Europe, sung my songs all across Canada, coast to coast. I seldom played the USA, too many guns. I do all the business arrangements myself. I book my own gigs, my travel, car and equipment rentals, and four star hotels. I enjoy the process. I have never been offered Japan, Australia, NZ, or Russia, but I would love to sing in those countries. I tend to play the same venues every six months, building a following in that location, but playing a different set of songs, each visit. Repeat ticket sales are the foundation of every artist. I have recorded in London, Nashville and LA, because I see these locations as controlled and comfortable.

It's wonderful recording away from home with their better, homegrown, players.

I have played as a solo, a duo, a trio, a quartet and the largest band configuration was seven. Guitars, piano, kit, violin, bass, synth, sax, and cello. All work, all were fun, all were challenging. My preferred line up was trio. Guitar, cello and orchestral percussionists. I insist on perfect sound, great gear, and the best soundman is essential. I never compromised in that department. Good players, good harmonies, good attitude. I vary the size with each year. It's more alive that way.

In Great Britain I had played Manchester, Brighton, Leeds and many other UK cities, but I had never played a show in the Big Smoke, in the Square Mile, in London. That was until the 19 day of September in 2006, when I headlined, a four act bill, on a Tuesday night, at the famous 12 Bar Club on Denmark Street, Soho. That night the sea met the horizon. I hit the perfect storm. I describe it as my happiest time on stage, ever. The best performance of my career. Ninety minutes of bliss.

For me, every concert is a battle between stage fright and joy. That night I found the elusive sweet spot. I felt in tune. I was in sync. The 12 Bar Club is just off Charing Cross Road and within touching distance of Trafalgar Square, in London's West End. The 12 Bar Club is a small room, 150 packed. It was sold-out that night. It was electric, eclectic, wild, and perfect. For me an historic autumn night in a musically perfect setting. The London Telegraph, voted the 12 Bar Club the *'Second Best Music Venue in the World'*.

Previous acts that graced that stage include Adele, her first London dates were at the 12 Bar Club. Roddy Frame, Rodney Crowell, and Billy Bragg. Jeff Buckley played an impromptu set at the 12 Bar before the launch of his debut album *'Grace'*. (1). The 12 Bar attracted a clientele that includes the famous, and it provided a unique platform for up-and-coming acts. It was possible to mingle with the likes of Noel Gallagher, Elvis Costello, or one of the New York Dolls. The venue's live room had great acoustics and is also soaked in history, possessing a Vicwardian balcony and a stage wall from 1642.

I booked the gig over the telephone a month earlier with Andy Lowe, a former DJ and Decca records employee, the impresario. Andy opened his arms to me after listening to a cassette tape that I mailed to his office. Six songs that showed the music that I would perform. I would headline, with three opening acts. My slot was scheduled for 10.15pm. I was thrilled.

All was in flow, London sang to me, I saw the sights, walked the streets and parks. However, on day three, I suffered a setback. My right knee locked whilst in the hallowed halls of Westminster Abbey. Ouch! Sharp focused discomfort. I now had a noticeable limp. A few weeks later I had knee replacement surgery in Vancouver. But for the time being I had to endure. I had to mentally compartmentalize this hiccup, focus on the gig, two days away. Aspirin, massage, rest. I soldiered on knowing that the set was the heart of the matter. I flew across the ocean for this spot. *'The Show must go on'*, a phrase originated in the 19th century circuses. I understood this theatrical credo, meaning to continue despite any problems.

The days slipped by and on September 19th the Orient Express arrived. Showday! I nervously headed out. Took the tube to Tottenham Court Road station. Arriving at the club at 6pm for soundcheck. The 12 Bar Club seemed empty. It was not. A solitary soul was sitting behind the soundboard, 19 year-old John. Alone in this dark, foreboding, and intimidating space

'I'm Barry Greenfield. Can we do a soundcheck please?'

''Ello Barry, I'm John, and that's why I'm here mate'.

The next words I spoke are a key to why I hit the sweet spot that night.

'John, I need your help tonight please. I want to be really loud. I mean really, really loud. I only have one guitar but make it intense. I need and want every word, in every song, to be clear to the audience'.

John, a true cockney, shone brightly. London folklore maintains that only those born within sound range of the Bow Bells are true Cockneys. John was the real deal.

'No problem Barry. Thats the way I do it. It's going to be really loud, and the audience will hear your words crystal clear mate!'

I smiled. I had found my partner in crime. I trusted John's attitude, his confidence, and his love for his chosen profession, soundman. The soundman is the key to the door when playing live.

My knee was screaming, and I had trouble getting up onto the stage. I had to step on a chair to climb up. Once in place the soundcheck was amazing. It all felt *better than comfortable*. *'Closer to fine!'* The two stage monitors served me well, and John was a total professional. A gift from the stars. My confidence bloomed. I was certainly loud, and the vocals cut like a knife.

'It sounds great out here Barry'

'It sounds great up here too John. See you at showtime. Thank you so much!'

I remain quiet and private when preparing for battle. I am nervous, anxious, and not very friendly. I rested my knee in a Denmark Street café.

The 12 Bar clientele were musically sophisticated and there to listen to the music and have a pint or two. Certainly not the situation in most venues where the music is secondary to the alcohol and loud conversations. I had found the type of venue I need. A room where music trumps chat and getting wasted.

At 10.15 I climbed on the chair, back on the stage, picked up my axe and hit an A major chord. The place vibrated. Thank you John.

'Hello London'.

I placed the capo on fret two and chugg-a-lugged a Greenfield rhythm, aggressive and dangerous in structure and tone, to get the audience's attention. Not as recognizable as Keith playing his open tuned Stratocaster saying, *'Start Me Up'*, but it worked in a similar fashion.

'Are you awake out there?'

I strode up to the well-used 12 Bar microphone. Stood there and stared. I was washed in white light, dressed in Johnny Cash black, and looking all my fifty-five years. I began.....

'Any Muslims out there?'

A few voices yelled yeah!

'Any Jews out there tonight?'

A few voices yelled yeah!

'Any Christians out there?'

A few voices yelled yeah!

'Well, this song is for all of you. It's for everybody who's thinking about God, Allah, Jesus or Buddha, Smooth Ambassador'.

It was a new one and I nailed it. It had power in the rhythm, a cross between *'Street Fighting Man'* and *'Alright Now'*. Soundman John had me filling every nook and cranny. The words were clear and succinct. I had seen through trump as early as 2006, in fact much earlier.

I was having supreme fun, right out of the gate. I had completed the first five minutes, and my tail was up.

Don't think much of Martha Stewart
The one who lied on the witness stand
Donald Trump is a thug and a bully
A one-armed-drummer-in-a-one–man–band
I'm the smooth ambassador

Tell the Rabbi Tell the Priest
Tell the Mullah Tell the Police
Tell the UN Tell the Pope
Here I come and I bring hope
I'm the one the world is waiting for
I'm the smooth ambassador

I shared with my new friends that I had flown in a few days earlier from Vancouver to play for them, and they cheered. The set felt like a steam train pulling out of Euston Station in London, and it gained momentum as we left the city, hitting full throttle as we approached Birmingham Station an hour plus later. The hour had no blanks. All my shots hit the mark like a bullet from a well known gun. The last song was *'New York is Closed Tonight'*, and I talked about its acceptances as a 9/11 commentary, although I composed it in 1969. The entire room vocally assisted me as they blasted out the tag la la la's and I was satisfied and done.

My eyes are hurting badly
I'm breathing through my nose
My white shirt is turning gray
I should wear plastic clothes
It's getting dark so early
So long before its night

And the neon freeway sign
Said New York is Closed Tonight

My t shirt was wet as if I had swum in it, face beet red, my knee still screaming, this man was a happy camper. They erupted.

'Encore'.

I thought I'd better not try to climb down from the stage, better to enjoy this rare moment where the energy circle with an audience was in overdrive mode. I had '*Landmines*' ready. It's a song that Celina Tuttle, the CEO of Mines Action Canada, had selected to use for her Landmine awareness campaign, I donated it, and Mines Action Canada incorporated it in their campaigns for many years. I shared the song's metamorphosis before playing it, explaining that Princess Diana motivated it's creation a few years earlier.

In 1997 Diana, Princess of Wales's did a landmine walk in Angola. It had a far-reaching impact, triggering a worldwide conversation that saw a turning point in the fight against the lethal devices. The photo shoot, by the press in attendance that day, created an evocative image, Diana wearing a protective visor and flak jacket, walking through a live minefield in Huambo, Angola.

Princess Diana visited Angola as a guest of the International Red Cross in January of 1997. The conflict had left the country contaminated by more than 15 million landmines. These hidden weapons, often scattered near towns and villages, were having a devastating effect, causing extensive civilian casualties, and hindering any effort at post-conflict recovery. At the time of the princess's visit, one in every 330 people in Angola had lost a limb.
(2)

The song was listened to in a kind of a hush. It's a hard song to sing live, but I was in London, and Diana motivated the songs birth.

I got a one legged man hopping down the street
A one armed girl hungry and weak
A blind young boy with dead-man's eyes
Another day gone in a hard life

You get the triggers from Poland
You get the casings from France
You can pay for them in Dollars
You can sell them for Rands

There are cheap ones from Calcutta
Or really big ones from Japan
They kill indiscriminately
Some go off in your hand

You never get a warning
Just a short sharp pain
And a heat flash
That burns every nerve in your brain

They left these things behind
Like someone leaves a tip
It's a comment on mankind
Its pure bullshit

And it's more than bad luck
So much more
Landmines

I remember the cheer that went up when I sang and emphasized *'It's pure Bullshit!'* in Landmines. They had been listening to the words of the song quietly and intently until then and that got such a big reaction from the politically astute crowd.

'Encore'

I felt spent after *'Landmines'*, but it was not a place to end. I thought *'what do I play?'* A great proverb that was first used in the Southern United States came to mind, *'if it ain't broke don't fix it!'* I played my opening song, *'Smooth Ambassador'* for a second time that night. This pass less aggressive, more contemplative. The emphasis on the thought behind the lyric, not the heavy, foot stomping rhythm that I had opened with an hour earlier. It worked like a charm. I had won the battle with my set, and with my encore I had triumphed in the war. Life was good.

Don't think much of Superman
Green Lantern never did nothing for me
I liked the Riddler
I liked the Penguin
Beating up Batman on my TV
I'm the smooth ambassador

I blame the stress, jet lag, poor sleep, and fractured knee, for lots of poor decisions that week. Andy Lowe asked if I would play again later in the week. Man, I would have loved to say yes, but I had flight plans.

I thanked the crowd profusely. The applause lingered. I got help getting down from the stage, and I grabbed a towel. I forgot to bring a clean shirt. A line of people were waiting for me. They wanted to say thank you and get an autograph, a smile, or a hug. I felt blessed and honoured. Two that waited patently in that line are memorable to me. The first was third in line. A girl in her late teens with her friend. She was a little too shy to make eye-contact with me, but said what she wanted to say,

'Next time you come to London, I'm bringing my mom. She'd love your singing and your songs Barry'.

About ten back from the young girl stood a short man with long grey hair flowing down his back. He was about seventy. He smiled and shook my hand,

'My whole life David Crosby was my favourite songwriter. Now its you!'

He asked for an autograph.

I still think back to my gig at the 12 Bar Club on Denmark Street as the most special live concert ever. I was given an opportunity to sing my songs for strangers, who became friends. Music heals. It did my heart and soul good to travel across the sea to sing.

Footnote:

'Ma Nishtana (Hebrew: מה נשתנה*)* *'Why is this night different from all other nights?'*

Many stars must align for such a synchronistic night to occur.

- *I was in England. Different audience. Different air.*
- *The right setlist. Twelve strong songs.*
- *I had a great sound man.*
- *I had a bone fracture in my right knee. The result of dealing with twenty four hour of pain was a release of stored energy. Boom!*
- *I really wanted to play. I felt like a taut elastic band. Once the elastic is at maximum stretch, and you let it go, it's a rocket to Venus.*

1. Pinnock, Tom (13 November 2015). "Jeff Buckley "was creating something bigger than the song"". *Uncut*

2. BBC https://www.bbc.com/culture/article/20240112-princess-dianas-1997-landmine-walk-i-come-with-my-heart

14

'My day in Auschwitz'. Five songs. 2019

Auschwitz talked to me.

I was introduced to the graphic visuals and the horrific details about *Konzentrationslager Auschwitz* at the tender age of seven. A young Jewish boy sitting, with my sister Suzan, in a matinee at the Gaumont Cinema, in Manchester, in the mid-1950's.

Auschwitz talked to me.

The cinema was a Saturday fixture for Manchester children. The Pathé News footage opened the afternoon festivities, and ran for eight minutes, with the average story lasting a minute. A typical episode began with a segment of '*hard*' news and wound its way down to '*softer*' news items as it progressed, usually ending with a recap of recent sports events. Sometimes The Football League First Division, the top division of English football until 2004 when The Premier League was introduced. Occasionally Canadian Ice Hockey, or American baseball would be featured. I loved them all, they gave me insight into other countries.

Pathé News was my introduction to global events. It set the pattern making me a news watcher, and reader. I maintained that habit until the trump presidency in 2016. At that juncture I ended my romance with news forever. News is not always 100% honest. Fake news has always been in the zeitgeist. I lived my life without knowing that. I had been fed propaganda for six decades by *Time* magazine, *The Globe and Mail, NBC, BBC, Al Jazeera English,* and the *Province* newspaper in Vancouver. The train had left the rails with trumpism having an affect on Global matters. It shook my foundation, and it still does, as we now endure a second term of danger.

Auschwitz talked to me.

The black and white footage, shown before the cliff hanger in the Gaumont theatre, intrigued young Barry. The history shared, absorbed by me, and it altered me. How could these grainy black and white images be real?

Auschwitz talked to me.

Poland opened the Auschwitz-Birkenau State Museum in 1979. This Museum had been designated as a World Heritage Site. Auschwitz is recognised as being the place of the largest mass murder in a single location in history. It is estimated that one point three million Jews entered, and one point one million Jews were murdered whilst the Camp was in operation. 1941-1945. *Konzentrationslager Auschwitz* connected with me, but I had no idea why.

In that sanguine theatre environment, my sister Suzan and I witnessed chilling images of the dead, dying and starving, living, and dying, in filth. Emaciated lifeless, and emaciated living souls, wide eyed looking into the camera lens, mouths asleep, no strength to talk, no energy to move. Broken, defeated, starved. The footage was filmed in 1945 when *Konzentrationslager Auschwitz* was liberated. The graphic scenes touched me, hurt me, frightened me. I would later, much later, discover that the Camp became the major site of the Nazis' Final Solution to the Jewish Question.

Auschwitz screamed at me.

Throughout my life I had read books about the Camp. I voraciously studied film about the Camp. I had thought deeply about the Nazis and the Final Solution. I had taken a deep dive into Adolf Eichmann. I studied Eichmann because he was tasked with facilitating and managing the logistics involved in the mass deportation of Jews to ghettos and extermination camps. Eichmann was captured, put on trial, and executed in 1962. He portrayed himself as a bureaucrat. He was a psychopath.

The arrival of YouTube greatly enhanced the amount of data available. Feature films such as 'The House on Garabaldi Street', 'Operation Finale', 'The Trial of Adolph Eichmann', and 'Denial' gave insight, in league with the literature available.

In May 1960, Eichmann was tracked down and apprehended by Israel's Mossad intelligence agency and put on trial before the Supreme Court of Israel. The highly publicized Eichmann trial resulted in his conviction in Jerusalem, following which he was executed by hanging on May 31st, 1962. I was eleven, but I felt a personal connection with the trial and resulting execution. His body was cremated and his ashes dispersed into the sea, outside of Israeli waters. I recall trying to understand what that meant, and the significance of that decision.

I had always thought I should, or indeed that I would, visit Auschwitz. I had talked about a visit with my daughter for decades. But Auschwitz is in Poland. It felt uniquely scary and threatening to me. And why should I go? Mexico, New York, Paris, Ireland seemed more important. Easier. Fun. So, the talk, though serious in nature, resulted in no action. Then in 2018 my daughter had an idea. A family trip to Europe, which would culminate at the Museum Auschwitz-Birkenau. What began as a family breakfast discussion, ended a month later, on a Lufthansa 747 flight heading for Frankfurt.

We were *The Griswold Family,* on a European vacation. My wife Lori, my son-in-law Graham, my daughter Macartney, and me. Five countries in an SUV. We began in Switzerland, a highlight. The first day we rode a gondola to the peak of the Alps (a bucket list thing for Barry). It was exceptional. The top of the world. Majestic. Sharing that experience with Lori, Macartney and Graham was brilliant. I was spiritually moved by the beauty we witnessed that afternoon.

After a five-day road-trip, that included beautiful Lucerne, Vaduz in Lichenstein, the Swarovski Kristallwelten Museum in Watten Austria, Vienna, and Salzburg, our trip of a lifetime terminated in Vienna. We spent that night absorbing the beauty of that great European capital, then we flew to Kraków, Poland. Our destination the Hotel Unicus, ul. Sw. Marka 20, Stare Miasto, Krakow. A boutique small hotel, on a lovely Polish street. Kind staff. Agreeable rooms. We arrived 6th April, 2019, booked for two nights. Macartney had planned, booked and organized the entire experience. It was choreographed beautifully.

Kraków, Poland, is the jumping off point to Auschwitz. It was similar to Napal's Camp IV, the last stage before a summit attempt on Mount Everest. The historic, local Tibetan name for Mount Everest is Chomolungma, also spelled Qomolangma, meaning '*Goddess Mother of the World'*. Once one departs from Camp IV, on the last push to the summit, on Chomolungma, the climber enters the death zone. Our Camp IV was Hotel Unicus. Our death zone was *Konzentrationslager Auschwitz.*

Auschwitz was close, I could feel the weight in the Kraków night air, the death zone in Poland was near. It was an uncomfortable weight. April 2019 was cold and damp in Kraków, Poland, a feeling of foreboding filled the night.

The alarm clock rang at 4am. We showered and gathered in the small lobby. We all had coffee, prepared by Unicus staff. The hotel had made four lunch bags for our excursion. Each bag contained an apple, a cheddar cheese sandwich made with Wonder Bread, a small juice box, orange flavour, and a single napkin. All neatly placed inside a brown bag. They looked like school lunches, but they did not have our names written on them. The hired car arrived promptly, as promised. We left at 6am prepared for a Polish picnic, but this day trip was certainly not a picnic.

We drove through Kraków as she was waking up to another day. Then a one-hour plus drive down a winding Polish country road, culminating in the large parking lot of Auschwitz-Birkenau. It was 7.20am. The Museum Auschwitz-Birkenau opened its doors at 8am. The driver was experienced and well trained. He drove people to Auschwitz, and then chauffeured them back, six hours later, five days a week.

Our driver detailed the Camp's history. The relevant dates, its size, its population. Softer facts about the Camp. His script was rehearsed. It was spoken with intent, to get the audience inside the car ready, warmed, prepared for the unique day that lay ahead. It was the identical speech and script that he had memorized for each commute, each working day, with his foreign visitors.

I sat in the front passenger seat. We all listened, riveted. I would later realize how his talk was perfect as an introduction for what was to come. He kept away from the horror, stood apart from the mayhem, and simply shared information without emotion. A history lesson.

To my right, 100 yards away, train tracks ran parallel to Kur Road, heading east from Kraków. I did not ask, and he never said, but the tracks from Kraków led in the direction of Auschwitz. From time to time, I stared at those train tracks. I have never researched whether those tracks are 80 years old. That mattered little. One could still see, hear, feel, the long rows of cattle cars slowly rumbling out of their numerous ports of call. Laden to the brim, overflowing, with human cargo. Squashed, hungry, thirsty, terrified, lost, human cargo. Many died from exhaustion, starvation, suffocation.

We arrived at 7:30 am. Daylight was looming.

Konzentrationslager Auschwitz had a parking-lot for the vehicles used by its visitors. Tour buses galore, cars a plenty, vans, RV's, all parked neatly like at a local mall. It was unsettling. I felt like a stranger in a strange land. I was completely present, but it felt dreamlike. We thanked Krzysztof the driver, and we arranged our pickup time and place, and then we walked through the gate. '*ARBEIT MACHT FREI*', work sets you free.

Krzysztof introduced us to Bart, our guide, who was waiting at the entrance of the Camp. A 33-year-old Pole, his grandparents were murdered at the camp. He became our voice of *Konzentrationslager Auschwitz*. Bart was serious, deep, intense and dark in nature.

Each member of the family received a personal headset. It had a microphone attached, for questions. He spoke in broken English. Our tour was private, only we four, and it would last six hours. Five peas in a pod, connected by Bart's unemotional, flat, accented voice. Under Bart's direction we remained in constant motion. Walking, moving, thinking, listening. The man's voice spoke with passion. A tour he hosted every work day, for the last three years, telling the world, or at least those that would listen, the story of the Holocaust. The history and horror of a Death Camp. Graphic, unfiltered, detailed. It became personal between my guide and me. Bart and I developed a repartee. A connection. I was the elder in the family group.

The day was grey, befitting our journey through the buildings and streets. A plot of land, enormous in size, that had been occupied by brutalized and dying Jews. The dead were always present, in the mud, in the barracks, awaiting work crews to remove the corpses. The walking dead were there the day we visited the site. I could feel, sense, see, what was invisible. The mud ground was now bone dry. But still one could imagine the smell and feel the filth, that was now replaced with manicured ground.

Lori, my wife, my partner, is gifted in many ways. We are each others shadow in so many circumstances. Lori has devoted a lifetime studying the countless methods one can employ to empower personal transformation for the collective well being. She offers insights about people, events and history that educate and illuminate. She is an author and speaker. In Auschwitz, Lori explained that over the years healers had visited the Camp, and that their energy-work, on the land in question, made it less dense, energetically, and therefore made the Camp *less challenging* for a 2019 visitor. We did not cry; it is a museum, and the experience felt like that. We were walking around dead souls. We were hearing silent screams. We were moved, but not to tears, but transferred to a deep place of aloneness. A personal and private place, that would be unique to every visitor. I was overwhelmed by the experience, and I felt privileged to feel it.

We stopped at the 'Death Wall', where thousands upon thousands of prisoners were shot by a firing squad, for no reason, or for any reason. This wall was adjacent to Block 11, the brick building used by the guards for executions and torture. Torture included being locked in a dark chamber for several days or being forced to stand in one of four standing cells '*Stehzelle*'. Punishment in these special compartments, one metre each, with a small hole for breathing. The Nazi's confined four prisoners, who were forced by the lack of space to remain standing all night for up to twenty nights, while still being forced to work during the day.

Unimaginable to me when I listened to Bart graphically describe the horror, the inhumanity. All I could think while frozen in place was '*it could have been me; it would have been me!*'. The pain, the fear, the reality went deep into my soul. I touched the 'Death Wall'. Its cold brick feel lingered inside me as I kept my right hand flushed against its hard surface for thirty seconds, absorbing memories of murder.

We walked through deserted barracks and saw the now empty bunkbeds that at one time were overcrowded, infested with lice, sprinkled with blood, mud and tears. I could imagine the rats, which were not there now, but where there then. The dying were everywhere, but nowhere.

The new arrivals at the camp, were stripped naked, either to be shaved and given camp clothes, or to be gassed. The Nazi selection was quick and based on the Jews ability to work. I imagined a drunk Nazi, or a smirking Ukrainian thug, sitting on a chair pointing right, or pointing left. Work. Gas. *Selektion* (selection) was the process of designating inmates either for murder or forced labour. First a separation by gender, and then a separation into either fit or unfit for work after a visual inspection or perhaps a question or two. Children under sixteen, and later fourteen, the elderly, women visibly pregnant, mothers who would not leave their children, the disabled, or anyone visibly weak or ill, were ineligible for '*selection*' and were summarily murdered.

We visited numerous rooms with glass partitions. One such room displayed suitcases with names, addresses and dates of birth written on them. Many survive, including the suitcases brought by Marie Bohm, Dr. Kurt Weilunger and Petr Eisler. Bart explained that from early 1942, when the mass gassing of Jews began, prisoners would bring their belongings with them, in the belief they were being resettled. The Germans allowed them to carry up to 100 pounds. The unwitting Jew brought food, alcohol, household items, utensils, clothing, medication, valuables, and professional tools all of which ended up in the Kanada warehouse.

Prisoners who worked in Kanada were known as the *Aufräumungskommando*. Working in Kanada was viewed as one of the best jobs in Auschwitz, because prisoners could procure goods for themselves and other inmates. The guards would freely take what they wanted from the enormous piles of property at their disposal. Valuables, jewelry, clothing, art. Vultures feeding from the carcass.

Other rooms with partitions displayed Jewish shoes, Jewish hair, Jewish eyeglasses, and many personal items.

Bart spoke about the Jewish Kapos, who beat their Jewish brothers and sisters, to gain an extra piece of bread, or maybe live a few weeks longer.

The Україна (Ukrainian) thugs who were brutal, for the sake of being brutal. The place stank of pain, sorrow, suffering. But mostly it reeked of inhumanity. The sad state of affairs that was to be repeated by Pol Pot, Idi Amin, Bashar Hafez al- Assad, and Kim Jong-Un, to name a few. We touched the walls of the gas chambers. The shower rooms. We stood on the ramp where the Jews disembarked from the train, for immediate selection. *'Sie havens see! Richts overclasses! You left! You right!'*.

These deportees were brought to Auschwitz crammed in wretched conditions. Transported in cattle wagons, arriving, after days of travel, at one of several dedicated trackside ramps. Most deportees were forced to walk, accompanied by SS guards and a car with a Red Cross symbol that carried the Zyklon B. Inmates arriving at night, or who were too weak to walk, were taken by truck.

Silently, feet moving, our hearts beating, but forever changed. Auschwitz One was complete. We walked out through the gate stunned, silent and drained. We now had a thirty-minute reprieve, before a ten-minute drive to Auschwitz Two, Birkenau Camp.

That thirty minutes was spent in the van. No talking. Not moving. We all consumed the food in the brown paper bag. It seemed odd to eat after the last few hours, but we did.

Bart returned, and our Krakow driver shuttled us to Birkenau. It was larger. Less but more. Two hours walking between destroyed barracks, each building had a story, Bart carefully filling in the blanks. He shared many personal tales about prisoners, tales that Bart had learnt in his training. Bart had spent two years in training before being able to lead a group of visitors. His details and passion were enormous, commendable.

My family and Bart stumbled through the rubble of one of the gas chambers. Destroyed by the fleeing Nazis, days before the Russian arrival. They foolishly thought that destroying the tool, would hide the tool. The crematoria consisted of a dressing room, gas chamber, and furnace room. The Camp crematorium ovens were in a word, overwhelming. The oven doors were open so that the visitor can view the size of the unit. They were large and built in a line to allow for the easiest loading of a body, and then the removal of the ash after incineration. A dreadful view. A hopeless, demeaning, cruel task for the prisoners selected to do the job.

The temperature was dropping, and our visit was ending. We walked out of Birkenau, shared a brief thank-you and hug with our guide, then we drove back to Hotel Unicus. Arriving as it grew dark.

I was full of knowledge, my heart was sad, my soul was altered. The day at *Konzentrationslager Auschwitz* was different to any day prior. I had lived sixty-eight years. Sharing that day with Lori, Macartney and Graham was priceless.

Lori and I left the kids in Kraków. They flew to Paris; we flew to Frankfurt. Three nights, at the Sofitel Frankfurt Opera. A hotel that was the equal to any hotel we had graced previously, an equal to the Sofitel New York. Luxury in Frankfurt felt odd after Oświęcim Poland. We sat on the king bed, looked at the opulence and wondered, and talked, about life.

We were in Germany, and it felt strange. We thought. We talked. We hugged. We sat in restaurants, or walked the *straßen von Frankfurt,* and we would notice residents that had lived as adults during the war. We saw, normalcy, grandparents, and we heard laughter. Three days of fog. We accomplished little. Walked and walked. Museums. Coffee shops. Early nights, Early days. We talked very little about that day.

I knew that I would write songs about *'My Day in Auschwitz'.*

I returned to my Canadian life where I became obsessed, reading about the camp. Book after book.

The best read was written by Laurence Rees, the former Head of BBC TV History Programmes. His detailed and informative book, *'Auschwitz the Nazis, and the Final Solution' (2005),* inspired me to create music and lyrics about my experience, My goal was to share my experience with those too young to have a deep understanding of the history.

I sought out *prisoners* who had survived the camp and emigrated to Canada. I interviewed them in person or on the telephone. I met their children, who are labelled second generation Auschwitz survivors. They told a story of how their lives had been impacted by living with parents who survived hell.

A year later I began to create. The first song was *'The Gate'.* I put grand piano on the track, it needed that formal sound. Then I added tympani, cello, electronic percussion, and chanting. I re-sang the lead vocal. *'The Gate'* was my way to capture that day-for eternity, for my family, and everyone who wanted to know.

I spent the next few months writing music and lyrics about the camp. I started ten, and finished five, and prepared a video-documentary for YouTube about *'My day in Auschwitz'.*

I spent six weeks in the studio recording the songs. It was certainly different than any other project. I enjoyed the catharsis of the work. Then I edited the five videos. I wanted each one to be unique. Each song stood alone. I used BBC footage of the Camp, stills and old archive film.

THE JEWS WHO WEAR THE YELLOW STAR (Five original songs about Auschwitz-Birkenau) by Barry Greenfield remastered 2024Auschwitz-Birkenau

https://youtu.be/zjLIcTCCcEk?si=ckCF7qSSnjK5Hysl

I submitted the documentary to Malka Weisberg at Auschwitz.org . He sent the video to Yad Vashem, the worlds largest Holocaust Museum in Jerusalem. Jeremey Weiss at Yad Vashem (New York), asked me if I would permit the museum to use the lyrics of 'The Gate' in their book to commemorate the 75th anniversary of the liberation of the camp. I agreed, and the book, a piece of art, has my words on page 51. An honour.

Tidbit one

Understanding the greatness that is Nashville 2007 and 2008

One of your mother's favourite sitcoms, from back in the day, *'The Golden Girls'*, had a wonderful theme song, *'Thank You for Being a Friend'*. An upbeat song with a positive melody and lyrics, written by Andrew Gold. Andrew told me that every year the show aired, he received a cheque from the producers for $25,000. He was a member of that miniscule group of musicians that made a substantial living, in the tough as nails music business. His entry point, the lucrative seventies. Much like The Pretenders, The Doobie Brothers, and Steely Dan, all entered the golden age, after The Beatles set the table.

Andrew, a dear friend, passed away in 2011. He was an uber talented musician. Best known for his hit *'Lonely Boy,'* and for being Linda Ronstadt's producer. Andrew sang, played guitar, drums and piano on Linda's biggest hit, *'You're No Good,'* and was a big reason for her enormous popularity and continuous success.

In 2007 I stayed at Andrew's home for a few weeks. I was recording in LA. One dark, warm LA night, on October 30th at 8.04pm a major earthquake hit the Valley. Walls moved; pictures fell. It was bedlam. We were shaken and scared. We waited until after midnight in the kitchen sipping on tea and waiting for any serious aftershocks. None came. Andrew feared a second visit by nature's fury. This resulted in the decision to move his family out of the earthquake zone and to Music City, Nashville, Tennessee, a friendly spot, with a population under a million.

In 2008 I planned a trip to Tennessee, to knock on doors in Music Row, the hub of the city's entertainment and publishing industry. I wanted to showcase my songs. Andrew was excited that I was coming, and he offered to book meetings for me. I was thrilled, and extremely grateful. *'Thank you for Being a Friend.'*

My first meeting was a co-write with Robert Ellis Orrall. Orrall had penned Number One singles for Shenandoah and Clay Walker and would later produce, and write, with a young up-and-comer, Taylor Swift. Writing in Music Row is like a meeting with an accountant or visiting the dentist. An appointment is booked. In this case we had a window to work in, 2pm to 5pm. I arrived a bit early. Robert walked in at two sharp. He told me that we should aim to get two songs started, three if we were lucky.

'What do you have in the pot Barry?'

'The Road Home' was a half-baked song idea I had. A verse, a chorus and the accompanying music. It was the story of a soldier coming back from Afghanistan. Robert liked it. We got to work. We finished it at 3.30pm. It was really good. But it now was a song about a travelling musician, missing his family and thinking about the road home. That was more of a Nashville concept, Robert taught me. We used my lyrics with the Orrall twist, my chords and melody that Robert enhanced beautifully. A giant of a writer. The next day we went into a demo studio and recorded *'The Road Home,'* I sang, Robert played the guitar.

Two months later it became a completed track on an LP on the Disney Label, Lyric Street Records. The recording artist was a 17-year-old wonder kid. They said that he played his guitar like Chet Atkins. I never heard the kid's version, but I spoke to his father twice on the telephone. A lovely man. I do not remember his name.

On my first call with Dad, he told me that his son loved the song and thanked me for offering it. Two weeks later, the second call. Dad phoned to inform me that his son was leaving the music business. His plan was to attend the University of Tennessee in Knoxville. He wanted to be a doctor. Apparently, the kid hated the idea of being in the music business. Leaves in the wind.

After two more rendezvous, with two female writers, both resulted in nothing of worth, I went to meet a mate at a deli, *'Noshvilles,'* I thought, what a great name, *'Noshvilles'*.

Chris Nole joined us at this swinging Southern deli. Early forties, friendly, a native of New Jersey. Chris and I hit it off. We talked for almost an hour. Music, the planet, sport. We exchanged e-mails.

Back in Vancouver I hatched an idea. I wrote to Chris.

'I am coming back to Nashville to meet with Capitol Records.'
'Would you be interested in recording a song with me in your home studio?'
'Love to!'

I returned to beautiful Tennessee a few weeks later. I rented a car and drove out to Brentwood, a Nashville suburb. He and his fiancé, now wife, Jennifer, had a welcoming home and a fully equipped studio in the loft. Perfect.

I played him my version of John and Paul's *'She Loves You.'* I explained how much I loved the lyrics, and that I felt it had always been overlooked. I wanted it performed straight from the heart, on a grand piano, softly sensitively and quietly. It would be sung by a single voice, mine. The *'yeah yeah yeah'* hook would not be sung but played by his right hand. Chris listened, showed me some touches, and proved that he understood my concept perfectly. Chris, who had been John Denver's pianist for many years, played like a virtuoso, with enormous sensitivity. World class. He nailed it. Right-out-of-the-gate. He understood me and I understood him.

It took us about three hours. We recorded it live, him playing, me singing. Then we added a synth flute and cello. It was perfect. We bonded.

Chris shared his John Denver memories and the great loss he felt at John's death. He called him Uncle John.

Before leaving Nashville I asked Chris to put together a budget. Four songs, a recording studio and a band. He sent it to me a few days later. We booked the studio, and I began to write and select the four songs. Over the next six months, I had four trips to Nashville and four recording sessions. We had enough songs in the can for a Greenfield LP.

The studio, Sound Emporium, was owned by Garth Fundis, best known for his work with Don Wiliams, Trisha Yearwood and Alabama. A great room.

The players Chris selected were three gentlemen, seasoned veterans. All possessed a work ethic par excellence. They would all kick in ideas about their parts. I encouraged an open session where their input was sought and respected.

-On guitar was Jack Pearson. A member of The Allman Brothers Band, and session player for the stars, Joe Bonamassa, Vince Gill, Jimmy Buffett, Earl Scruggs and others.

-On stand-up bass, and electric bass, was Dow Tomlin. A seasoned Bassist out of Nashville who has toured and recorded with Wynonna Judd, The Judds, Little Big Town, Faith Hill and others.

-On the drums was Chris Brown. After arriving in Nashville, from New York, in 1992, Chris became one of the most sought-after jazz drummers in the South.

-On piano, Hammond organ, accordion and synth, was my co-arranger, Chris Nole. Chris has collaborated with the best in the business over his many years in music. From Faith Hill to John Denver to Travis Tritt to Shelby Lynne to Don Williams.

The four trips were identical, all about six weeks apart. This symmetry, and discipline of habit, I believe enhanced the work, and the resulting ten songs we recorded. If I removed surprises and kept it simple it helped. I was in a foreign land, with world class talented players, and I needed to reduce challenges, and simplify what I could, for me to run hot. These seasoned players were the cream of Nashville. They were all used to a focus and a clarity of vision for the writer/performer. My intention was not to disappoint that expectation.

Day one. Wednesday morning. I would fly from Vancouver and arrive in Nashville that night.
    Day two. Thursday morning, Chris would pick me up at 9am, at my hotel, the Brentwood Suites, we would grab a coffee and a muffin and head back to his studio in Brentwood. We worked until 6pm, with an hour lunch break. We would chat about the world, love, music, and our journeys. In the working hours we arranged four songs; tightened arrangements; wrote guitar parts, bass parts, drum parts and Chris's keyboard parts for all four songs that were to be attempted the next day. I would work on my phrasing and my entry points. I would alter the lyrics to fit the arrangement. When

we were satisfied, I would head back to the hotel for a little TV and a lot of sleep.

Day three. We went straight to the Sound Emporium studio, arriving at 9.30am. I would meet the boys in the parking lot, to help them carry their gear into the room. They loved that aspect of our relationship. The guy paying, helping carry the gear of the guy playing. Drums, amps, guitars, all would take a few trips. I believed that act of kindness helped with the amazing chemistry that we five built over that year. All the players made themselves available for each date. They all wanted to do it. I felt blessed. We have all stayed in touch to this day.

The session began at 10am sharp. The boys sipping coffee from Styrofoam cups in the control room as we listened to an mp3 of my song. One at a time. The musicians' eyes firmly fixed on the Nashville chords charts, prepared by Nole, a series of numbers (almost a code) humming and tapping their fingers, preparing. Then we entered the studio, and it was like they knew the song. It amazed me every time. We followed this process for each song we recorded.

The first candidate with my new Team was a song I had written about my daughter in 2007. It captured a sunny day I spent with her at age eight. Macartney and I are very connected. Extremely close, and we help each other as we walk through life. I composed this song for the lads to interpret in Nashville. It had a gentle country feel and although it was not a *'cowboy hat'* song, it had a nod to music city. It was called *'Lil Angel'*. We listened to my version in the control room, and then we took our positions and what they played literally *blew my mind*. The way these great players understood. Cared, and nailed it, amazed me. I had only felt that way once previously, that time being in Hollywood with Larry Carlton, Joe Osborn, Larry Knechel and Jim Gordon in 1973 in my *'Blue Sky'* sessions.

I'm walking in sunlight
With a smile on my face
And Little Angel on my shoulder
Dressed in brocade and lace
I'm watered by rain I'm heated by sun
I'm alive I'm ok

And Little Angel you're the one
Makes me feel this way
I see a fingernail moon
In an endless sky
And Little Angel
You're the reason why
Like every fish in the sea
And every bird in the sky
The secret is to learn
How to share
There's music in the wind
And sweet colitis in the field
And lil angel there's magic in the air
I'm wearing red shoes
Got gas in my car
And six new strings
On this old guitar
It's all because of you

© *2007 Barry Greenfield*

We would complete three music beds, the rhythm section, lead guitar, bass solo and rough vocal work, by 1pm. The afternoon and early evening, I would add my vocals to the three band tracks. My favourite part of the day. Then we did a fourth song. Just as a duo, me and Chris. Live. Then Chris and I would insert overdubs on all four songs. More piano, Hammond B-3 organ. Then a rough mix. Our day concluded about 7pm.

    Day Four, I flew home. I would spend the night in Minneapolis. It was a good place to sit still, rest, and recharge after three days of intense work. My hotel was across the freeway from the Mall of America in Bloomington Minnesota. It opened in 1992, and is the largest mall in the United States, the largest in the Western Hemisphere. Lots of nothing to see. But it became part of my routine. I would buy a present for my daughter on each visit. An article of clothing that I hoped she would enjoy. I generally was successful.

    Chris would mix the songs in his home studio and send me the mixes. He wanted my approval on the final sound-level, blend and effects. Plus, little tweaks that were always required to make the tracks shine.

'*Exposed Soul,*' my sixth LP, was complete. I picked the ten songs I thought ran best together.

Next, a photo shoot in Joshua Tree National Park. My concept for the artwork was a homage to my favourite Dylan record, '*Blood on the Tracks.*' To this end I hired a graphic artist that lived in Minneapolis. She did a lyric book insert, and a fabulous job on the front and back cover. It is my only gatefold LP. It is beautiful to the eye.

I did spend some time walking the streets of downtown. It is a southern US city. It is jam-packed with Country Music wannabees who are seeking a seat in the train car headed for the sky. Every café, every bar, has an act singing their hearts out, hoping, praying, that someone will walk in who could make a difference. Me, I never asked if I could participate. I probably should have asked and maybe sang a song or two. I am shy and I could not find the fortitude to seek it out. Nashville is a magnet for talented players. Lots of work. Live and in the studio. Nole came from New Jersey. Brown came from NY. They stayed in Nashville.

I loved being there. The studio was first class. I found working with musicians who had played with the cream the day before wonderful. They were happy to help me achieve my vision.

'*Exposed Soul*' is cohesive because it is a band album. Five players listening to each other and concentrating on making it good. Dave Kell, my dear friend, roadie, and partner in crime, for over two decades, has always thought it was my most cohesive ten songs.

Working in London, LA, Toronto and Vancouver were all interesting, but Nashville was the best. Simply the best.

Footnote:

My Nashville experience in 2008 was an enormous success. The music made, with that band, Pearson, Tomlin, Brown and Nole, was rewarding and satisfying. The growth that I had in how best to use a recording studio was significant.

But the most important gift I received in Tennessee was a lifetime friendship with Chris Nole. Priceless. Chris spent many years by the side of John Denver. A more talented man I cannot think. In his field John was special, and extremely unique. Working with Chris I could sense that he learnt a lot from all the artists he has helped. Chris is a strong a talent as I have ever shared a song with.

The environment where music is written, recorded, or performed plays an enormous role. Artists are sensitive souls, and a warm, peaceful, professional surrounding helps the art immeasurably Sound Emporium, and the lads made it shine.

Tidbit two

Some collaborations are platinum. Some collaborations are tin

Sunday morning is a mellow time in the sweetest day of the week; a day when time slips by ever so slowly. Slower than the other six. It was noon, the telephone rang. It was October 10th, 2004.

'Hi, Barry Greenfield, please'.
'This is Barry'
'Hi it's David Sancious. I am in Vancouver on tour with Sting. We played last night at General Motors Place. This morning a close friend played me your 'King of the Wolves' CD. I loved your songwriting. She had you number and I thought I'd give you a call'.
Polite, direct, and extremely flattering, but I thought it was a prank. I had been '*punked*' before.
'Who's calling please?'
'David Sancious'.

I knew that name. David Sancious was the keyboardist in Bruce Springsteen's E Street Band. The wonderful player on the Boss's first three LPs. I especially loved the Hammond organ and piano blend, both instruments played soulfully, by Sancious, and Danny Federici. Although I had never been a fan of Bruce's voice, I did love the E Street Band. The rock solid drummer, Bruce's guitar, a deep bottom end on the bass, and the melodic sax player, Clarence Clemons.

David had toured with Eric Clapton, Peter Gabriel, Jack Bruce, and Jon Anderson. He was a crucial part of Springsteen's *'Greetings From Asbury Park* and *'The Wild, the Innocent and the E Street Shuffle,* and *'Born to Run',* but he was also the only one to actually live on E Street, giving the band its name. Why would this man telephone me? I wondered who was behind the charade. I decided to be cautious. I just could not believe that David Sancious had my number or would call me to say he liked my latest CD.

'David, let me call you back, may I have your number please'.

He gave me a telephone number with an area code I did not know. 845. I called BC Tel, and they informed that area code 845 covers all or parts of several counties in the Eastern United States. I called it back after two minutes had passed. To my amazement the voice answered. It was him, David Sancious. I nervously explained my trepidation and he understood.

David explained that a financial planning client of mine, Jacqueline, was a close friend of his, and had been for many years. Jacqueline had dated the British musician Seal, and David played piano in Seal's touring band. David was in Vancouver, so she invited him to her home for a Sunday home cooked breakfast. After breakfast Jacqueline played him *'King of the Wolves'*. David said that he loved it and mentioned three songs on it, *'King of the Wolves'*, *'No-one Here is Getting Out Alive'* and *'Something Beautiful'*.

We discussed the three songs. He laughed when I shared that I written *'Something Beautiful'* because I loved George Harrison's *'Something'* and Billy Preston's *'You Are So Beautiful'*. I wrote the song in 2003, but I am now convinced every word, in that song, is about meeting Lori a decade later. Time need not be sequential. It was a song that I had sung regularly in my show.

> *Some days at night I stay up till sunrise*
> *When morning has broken, all I think of is you*
> *I was hoping you might put a light in your window*
> *So, I could be shown the path I must take*
> *That leads to your home I hope I'm not late*
> *Something felt good something felt right*
> *Something felt real when we met last night*
> *Something beautiful, something beautiful*

The conversation lasted 30 minutes. David shared a few lovely stories about Springsteen, calling it his happiest years. He quit the E Street because he grew tired of the style of arena rock Bruce wrote. David thought Sting left a lot to be desired. It was the only time in his career that he had to hold out for a fair salary and per diems. He was happy with the music, but not the business of Sting. He seemed eager for the tour to end.

We closed the wonderful call with David saying that he would buy my CD and call me in a few weeks, when he arrived home in Woodstock, New York.

True to his word David called and asked if I would be interested in collaborating with him. I did not hesitate, and a week later, in early December, I was flying east to Toronto on Air Canada. In Toronto I boarded a small commuter flight, 30 seats maximum, that was headed to Albany, New York.

Waiting at the luggage carousel was David, and soon we were in his Black SUV driving to Woodstock, the home of Dylan from 1965 to the early seventies. Dylan's family house was on Ohayo Mountain Road, and it was there many of his songs from that time frame, were created. Woodstock was also the area where The Band lived and recorded in the house known as *'Big Pink'*. I was excited to be going to such an energetically creative town in Northern New York.

Deep snow was ever present on the 90- minute drive from Albany, giving us time to connect. The music in the SUV was primarily British Invasion. Cream, Stones, Hendrix, Animals, Beatles, Donavon, mixed in with some Dylan,Raiders, Five Americans, and Sam the Sham. I loved every three minutes of the drive from Albany to Woodstock. He was playing my playlist. Playing it loud, it added to the ambience and provided us warmth on this cold New York afternoon. It was obvious our musical roots were similar. He a devout Cream and Hendrix man.

Arriving at his home, I met his charming wife, Kiran Ramgotra Sancious. Their home was spacious, beautiful and comfortable. Nestled in the woods and far from neighbours. Idyllic. He had taken his E Street money and invested wisely.

Without taking a breath, he said, *'Want to see the Studio Barry?'*

The studio was a large single room. About a thousand square feet. Tidy. Spotless. Laid out perfectly. Huge windows covered one wall. The view was all trees. Covered in snow. A Woodstock Christmas card. Perhaps ten keyboards, ranging from a Steinway to a cheap sixties' organ. Synths. Drums. Cords, cables and gadgets, all neatly placed in order. Surgical. Ten guitars. David shared a personal triumph with me. He told me that Clapton allowed him to play the "Layla" riff in concert, apparently a rare honour.

In addition, he had extraordinary recording gear. Microphones galore. An extraordinary guitarist and pianist. A musician's musician.

We went straight to work. Shoes off. I picked up a Sancious guitar and I played him *'Summerville'*. I had the whole song. E minor, A minor, B7. We doodled for 30 minutes, and when completed, he had improved the chords, tempo, feel and song. It was now sophisticated, smooth and jazzy. I was gobsmacked. I loved singing it. A sexy lyric about outdoor sex, he made music that fit the message that I had written. It still was a root 12-bar song, but his chords were more literate, older, wiser and more beautiful. It was one of the most exciting songwriting collaborations I had ever experienced. Gouldman was brilliant. Orral was talented. Bachman had chops. But Sancious was good enough for Springsteen, Beck, Clapton and Bruce. I felt blessed.

We fell asleep last night on the beach at Summerville
With a warm n' gentle breeze in my face
I made love to you the way you like me too
Delicious flavors I still can taste
In Summerville on the beach
We woke up with daylight holding each other tight
I found your foot inside my shoe
You made love to me for eternity
The way that lovers ought a do
In Summerville on the beach

Dinner made by Kiran was vegetarian, flavourful and curry. She was a professional chef. I slept in a small, cozy, room on the main floor. I awoke at six am and they joined me at seven. Fruit and music for breakfast, and back in the studio by nine am.

I suggested we write a song from scratch. We did. The song was *'Beautiful'*, and it was solid. It had a good hook, but it was not a survivor. Try as I may, and David loved it, I could not connect. We then did a third song, *'Maybe Yes, Maybe No'*. It had a Motown feel and I loved writing it. I wrote the lyric for a duo, and we each sang fifty precent. Harmonizing in the chorus and fade.

I will be gone soon but I will visit you
Perhaps as a starling outside a window
I will sing you a birdsong, listen for me darlin'
Maybe yes, Maybe no

Three songs complete. Now we will record them on my last day in Woodstock. It was wonderful watching him play piano, organ, accordion and guitar. *'Beautiful'* was all David as I could not find it. I played two guitars on each song, and I sang all the leads, except for our duet. The harmonies took a while, because we aimed for perfection, and the recording day took ten hours. An exciting ten hours.

David and I stayed up late. Talking until three am. He told me how much he respected and loved Bruce. He left the E Street Band to pursue solo work, and other opportunities, and he grew tired of the life. He went to Bruce's house to share his decision, and as with all things Springsteen, *'No problem man, I understand'*. We talked about David's love for Hendrix and all things Cream. He shined when he spoke about touring with Eric Clapton. I explained how songwriting was my avenue, not perfecting my instrument. We became friends. We still are.

I flew home a happy camper, with three new demos. Life is good.

I waited three years before I recorded *'Summerville'*. It's a key track on Nashville's *'Exposed Soul'* and David Sancious wrote the arrangement for my Nashville band. It's a song, and recording, I am very proud to have created.

'Summerville' written by Greenfield and Sancious
On YouTube https://youtu.be/KgcLmQsT-qc

Footnote:

David Sancious is brilliant. He helped Clapton, Sting, Seal and countless others sound better. Add Barry Greenfield to that list.

Chatting intimately, about big names, with David Sancious (he played with Eric Clapton , Peter Gabriel, Seal, Springsteen, and more), and Shane Fontayne, (he played with McCartney, Springsteen, CSNY, Jackson Browne and more) only reinforced a belief that I had already learnt, on my journey to Blue Sky, (sharing time with Kenny Rogers, Nilsson, Jimmie Haskell, Larry Carlton, Cher and more). The Big Ones are almost all nice, generous, kind, grateful and humble in their own way.

Tidbit Three

My weird, short Dylan tale, Sound Emporium Studios, Nashville September 20, 2007

In the 1958 an America TV series *'Naked City'*, ended each episode with a narrator intoning the iconic line:

'There are eight million stories in the naked city. This has been one of them'.

I have many stories on *'my journey to Blue Sky'*, not eight million, but a score or more. One such story is about Bob Dylan. It will be brief, and I acknowledge, it is inconsequential.

10am. Me, and my four prestigious Tennessee studio giants, are sitting in the control room. I am playing and teaching them the first song that day, a smooth jazz piece that I cowrote with David Sancious, keyboardist of the E Street Band, a song called *'Summerville'*. A lovely piano song about a beach on Nova Scotia that I had visited.

> *We fell asleep last night on the beach at Summerville*
> *With a warm n' gentle breeze in our face*
> *I made love to you the way you like me too*
> *Delicious flavours I still can taste*

I add for clarity, that these four musicians, all play with Country greats, such as Garth Brooks, Dolly Parton, Brooks and Dunn, and Trisha Yearwood. They are not the starstruck type. Mostly.

A well respected man, the studio owner, a producer of hits, an original *Nashville gangster*, and a man who was always kind to me, Garth Fundis enters 'B'. *'Hope you don't mind my interruption Barry, but I got some news for y'all, and I have some rules to explain.*

He began,

At noon Bob Dylan will arrive at Sound Emporium. He will be working in Studio A, all day. Bob's manager has explained how Bob will be treated, and I expect us all to respect and adhere to these requests, please and thank you.

-No one talks to Bob. Not hello. Not I love 'Tangled Up in Blue'. No, I love your hat, Bob! Nada!
-If anyone talks to Bob, Bob will leave the studio. That was made crystal clear to me. He will depart the premises.
-If you see Bob, you don't see Bob.
'I know that I can rely on y'all to help me make his visit work, because we want him back. Any questions? No! Ok, enjoy your day, and thanks.'

Garth was gone.

For some reason it made sense. It feels weird and over-the-top writing it now, but in Studio B, Garth was so on point, and deadly serious. We understood it, and that was it. We got to work recording '*Summerville*'.

Shortly after 12.20pm we began to hear the muffled sound of a band playing in 'A'. The Hammond organ was evident. Dylan! We continued. After two pm we began drifting off to the men's room, about twenty minutes apart. Everyone did it. The band, the engineer, the assistant, and me. We all wanted to see Bob in person. In the next 4 hours I made three trips. Most did. No Bob. We all reported back with each visit, either smiling '*no*', or nodding '*no*'.

At 5.15pm I made my third trip. The door to studio 'A' was wide open. I stood there and said '*hello*?', No answer, I walked in. 'A' was huge. All of Dylans gear was in place, but no players anywhere to be seen.

'*Can I help You?*' came a voice from the doorway.

Busted!

'*Hi, I'm Barry Greenfield. I'm working in 'B', and I wondered in to feel the energy in the room, sorry*'.

'*They're gone*'

He was the studio 'A' engineer, and without request, he proceeded to share the events of the day.

'*We were told that Bob was playing two nights at the Ryman Theatre. This was day two, the afternoon before the second show. They arrived underground in three vans, Came up in the internal private elevator. The were here for five hours. I engineered. The sounded amazing. I mean out of this world. It was his road band. I have no idea if they were rehearsing, recording, jamming or just having fun. The manager took every trace of what was on tape. Didn't leave me a note.*

Dylan never left 'A', not even a bathroom break, never said thank you, or hello. Drank from a thermos he had. Spoke minimally to the band. It was wonderful, yes, but like nothing I have ever experienced'.

I asked the engineer where Bob stood. I stood there in front of the fender twin amp. The microphone was still in place. I sang a line from *'Blowin' in the Wind'*.

'the answer my friend is blowin' in the wind
The answer is blowin' in the wind'.

I went back to 'B'. Shared the tale with my Nashville partner, Chris Nole, and the engineer, all the others had left. We went back to work. I sang the vocal on *'Summerville'*, then back to the hotel.

I saw and spoke to a few famous musicians in that studio over my five trips to Nashville. Joan Baez, at that time she was 66, an elder. She was open, talkative, and warm, we enjoyed a coffee standing and chatting. Kenny Chesney, who sang a great song, *'No Shirt, No Shoes, No Problem'* , a song written by Casey Beathard in 2002. We talked about Nashville, fame, and English Football. He too was relaxed and normal. He had an entourage of band, women, and assorted hangers on, of about fifteen. They were all eating take out in the small lobby of the studio. It was different and yet seemed natural. The Studio was always friendly, and nothing seemed inappropriate.

I am pleased I spoke to Joan and Kenny, and a few others, I am a friendly guy, and I love talking music. But I would love to have sat in a soft easy chair in that studio lobby and talked to Dylan about songs, the earth and Gibson guitars. I guess over his six decades of fame too many have thought that Bob wanted to talk, when all Bob wanted was peace, quiet and normalcy in his working day.

A few years later I hired a guitarist who had previously played ten nights with a touring band who opened the show for Dylan. One day he saw Bob sitting at a picnic table eating a burger from the food-truck. He broke the rule, walked up to Bob, and asked if he could share the picnic table and eat his burger. They talked baseball for twenty minutes. It was normal just like you and me talking about our children in an airport lounge. We are all one, Lori explains it so well. Ask her.

Footnote:

I have a theory that brilliant humans may be alien. How do they get so brilliant? Pyramids? the physicist J. Robert Oppenheimer? Stonehenge? George Harrison? Notre Dame? Grace Hopper? Shakespeare? Einstein? Jane Austen? Marie Curie? Lennon? Amelia Earhart? Rosa Parks? Anne Frank? McCartney? Da Vinci? Dylan?

Tidbit four

Graham Nash and Shane Fontayne Tarrytown NY 2016

Shane Fontayne and I have shared a bond for almost a decade.

My Californian friend, via London, Shane Fontayne has shared his guitar magic with the likes of Paul Simon, Rod Stewart, Crosby, Stills and Nash, and Springsteen. Lately, for the last decade, Shane has been partners in crime with Graham Nash touring the world as a duo. The gig he was born to do. Shane Fontayne is best known for when he went viral in 2012, as bandleader, and playing lead guitar at the Kennedy Centre Honors, with Heart, as they interpreted Led Zeppelin's *'Stairway to Heaven'*. The three living members of Led Zeppelin, Plant, Page, Jones, sat next to Michelle and Barack Obama in an opera box, a small, separated seating area, listening, watching, as Shane, the hired gun, executed. The pressure on the performers must have been enormous. Shane and his friends, plus choir, plus strings, plus horns, played what I consider the best cover song ever.

In the autumn of 2016 Shane called me from Thousand Oaks, his home in California. He was waiting for the road crew to arrive, to collect his guitars, amplifiers, and other road gear. He was leaving for a fifteen-day East Coast tour with Graham Nash. We had collaborated as writers, and we had recorded songs, but we had never met. So, we planned a NY meeting. The cherry on the cake would be me attending a Nash concert at the historic Tarrytown Hall. He described it as beautiful hundred-year-old theatre. A week later, on 4 October 2016, I am flying on the red-eye non-stop to JFK. The adventure had begun.

Graham Nash, and his long serving partner, David Crosby had had a falling out, and Shane had occupied that seat ever since. A feud that began in 2013, with Crosby blaming the '*inaccuracies* and '*misinformation'* in Nash's memoir as the cause of their argument.

Crosby said:

'I was very unhappy about it. It's a very shallow, very self-serving book – and full of BS. Chock-full.'

Crosby died in 2023. They never buried the hatchet.

Sunrise at Kennedy airport, New York, and a $55 cab ride to Grand Central Station. A Wednesday morning, and I am watching the big apple wake-up. It was chilly, noisy, and alive. Tired yes, excited definitely. I had two hours to kill. First, Starbucks, then I spent an hour in St. Patrick's Cathedral. I needed to sit in the quiet. The ornate, pristine, soulful, empty cathedral was perfect. I closed my eyes. Meditated and reset. My train ride to Tarrytown took forty-five minutes. A comfortable commuter train. I felt like a resident of the Big Apple travelling with my neighbours.

I showered at the Sheraton, had a brief power nap, then Shane and I spent the afternoon in the Sheraton coffee shop. It was a very relaxed chat.

We had written and recorded original good quality songs. One, '*The Bravest Boy*', ballad written about Michael Bublé's son, who faced a health challenge magnificently, and eventually beat it.

When I have to cry, I let it flow, and I think about you
It's you and I, earth and sky, and I know there's one thing to be true
I melt when you smile
And say Dad I'm ok
You are the bravest one
An inspiration to me
You are the bravest boy

Another song came after watching *'Hell or High Water'* a great movie about banks and poverty in Texas, I titled it *'TEXAS 1980'*.

FOR LOVE AND MERCY
I GET HOME DIRTY
I WORK THE RAILROAD
AND NOTHING MORE

GOT DESERTED
THE BABIES SCATTERED
NOTHING MATTERS
THAT'S FOR SURE'

LIFE DON'T SCARE ME
GOD DON'T KNOW ME
A LONELY CHURCH PEW
WITH A WOODEN FLOOR

1980 DEEP IN TEXAS
NOTHING CAN SAVE ME
1980 DEEP IN TEXAS
NO ONE CAN HEAR ME

DAY TO DAY
NIGHT TO NIGHT
PAY TO PAY
FIGHT TO FIGHT

1980 DEEP IN TEXAS

Writing together creates a certain synergy that must be in place to make good music. Meeting face to face seemed natural. No surprises at all. Its always nice when I get to hang with another musician. It's a natural bond. The three hours we spent in that café was time well spent. We dug deep into our English youth, our love for various artists, and our love for our wives and children. I have great respect for this man, and I am proud to call him friend.

It was time for soundcheck. A brief soundcheck is all the duo needed. Then we continued our chat over bowls of mushroom soup. We then separated, so that he could prepare for the performance. I walked the streets, loving the small town feel that was ever present in this New York hamlet.

I arrived at the Tarrytown theatre at 7.30pm I took my third-row seat. The room was 80% full. About six hundred people. Shane and Graham walked out at 8pm. The first set was one of the most enjoyable concerts I have ever attended. Two guitars, two voices, a piano at times. *'Marrakesh Express', 'Cathedral', 'Military Madness', 'Our House',* ending the set with *'Simple Man'*. Perfect. Intermission. I stayed in my seat. Thinking about the music I had absorbed. Then out from the wings came Dave, Nash's road manager, the man who gave me my ticket and backstage pass earlier. He was moving like a bullet from a well-known gun. Looking rushed, he looked at me and said,

'What are doing Barry?' 'Graham wants to meet you!'

I am a shy man, and backstage is something I avoid. But…I stood up and followed him through the side door to the backstage area. Nervous.

Dave yelled to his boss across the room.

'Graham, I got Barry.'

Graham Nash was 75. He looked healthy. Lean. Casual. Smiling. Grey. A senior. Dave ushered us into a private room, then disappeared. The two of us standing in an empty room that felt like it had not changed in a century. Graham was relaxed and happy,

'Hello Barry, thank you so much for flying from Vancouver. Shane has told me all about you, and I thought we should meet'.

I told him how much I enjoyed their first set. How much I thought that Shane brought to the night. He agreed with me. We talked about the Hollies, my second favourite British Invasion band. We chatted a bit about the changes in Manchester, where we were both born. He asked me about my friendship with Graham Gouldman, who wrote the Hollies hits, *'Bus Stop*' and *'Look Through Any Window'*. The last time he saw Gouldman was in 1966. I filled him in. We were both big fans of 10cc. Nash told me the story of how he, Allan Clarke, and the Hollies manager went to Gouldman's home to listen to Graham's songs. I knew the story from the Gouldman's perspective. Graham's mom, Betty, had explained it to me over a sandwich one day. The details were identical. Nash asked me about my songwriting, adding that Shane had played some of my tunes for him. It was a lovely exchange.

Then a weird thing happened. Nash called over his sound tech and lighting tech. He told them that he would be starting the second set with *'Bus Stop'*, and that they should make the needed changes. Both men scampered off to prepare. Intermission bells rang and Graham excused himself and was gone. Shane mouthed,

'See you after the show.'

I spent the next five minutes with Amy Grantham. Graham's fiancé, now wife. She is a well-respected NY photographer, and we talked about how much we both liked the late Linda McCartney's work. She shot outstanding black and white photographs.

Back to my seat. Set two. Nash and Fontayne reappeared. Nash mentioned that:

'well known Canadian songwriter Barry Greenfield has joined us tonight. I would like to dedicate the next song, 'Bus Stop' to Barry'.

'Bus stop, wet day, she's there I say, please share my umbrella.'

Nash has such a smooth high-flying tone. Fontayne played the guitar licks with grace. I smiled. The second set was filled more solid Nash hits. *'Woodstock'*, *'This Path Tonight'*, *'I Used to be a King'*, *'Wild Tales'*. He ended the set with Neil Young's masterpiece *'Ohio.'* Back for an encore he sang his signature song, *'Teach Your Children'*. The Crowd sang every word with this great duo.

I met Shane outside on the corner as planned. We headed to a Tarrytown bar for a farewell brandy. We talked about the set. I am sure that Shane's role is entirely different than Crosbys. But both were so important to Nash's vision.

The entire twenty-four hours was brilliant. As Stevie Winwood wrote, *'When you see the chance take it!'* . I walked back from the bar to the Sheraton. Slept well. Rode the rails back to JFK. I then flew back to reality, always happy to be with Lori.

Footnote:

I came home different. I learnt a great deal from Nash. How to communicate on stage better, how to focus on being relaxed when on stage, and how to be real when sharing my heart. Graham Nash is the real deal.

Shane used nine instruments that night. Various acoustic and electric guitars, mandolin and balalaika. His contribution was magnificent. Graham played an acoustic and piano.

Tidbit five

Taylor Hawkins and David Grohl

August 2018, Lori and I were on holiday in Kaanapali, Maui, loving our Sheraton room, for ten, sun soaked, mellow, days. A luxury, much anticipated escape. At some point each afternoon, I would go back to the room, leaving Lori to read by the pool, and I would work on my new Maui song, *'Goodbye Baby'*. It was day seven of our getaway, when we were told, by a waitress in Lahaina, that Hurricane Lane would hit landfall in Maui on day eight, the next day!

Hurricane Lane would bring strong winds to Maui and a torrential rainfall. After it ended Lane became the wettest on record in Hawaii, with peak rainfall accumulations of 58 inches (1,473 mm). We decided to flee, and head back to Vancouver, BC. We got the last two seats, on the last WestJet flight out, as it was explained to us by the WestJet agent. Angels protecting again. It was a scary, real life moment; we were relieved that we had avoided the terror that was coming. Home safe, recovering, from what we had never experienced before, or since, a tropical storm.

As September bled into October I decided to record. I wondered where? The first cases of COVID-19, in Wuhan, China were still a year away. I had cultivated a friendship with a great guitarist in the UK, Adrian Woodward. Adrian and I decided to record two songs in Turnpike Studios in London. I was off and running, excited to have a new challenge.

First up, my Maui song, *'Goodbye Baby'*. A dark song about a marriage crumbling into pieces. A song composed by a happily married man, in the most positive, idyllic spot, I know, Kaanapali. Some songs are not one percent real, like some books are all fiction. The lyric was about impending doom, a couple heading bullet fast into divorce. Many have felt that ache. The heart damaged. The soul burnt. It made for a solid story and a good Greenfield tune.

WE'RE COLD AND BLUE
CAN'T TAKE NO MORE
NOTHING LEFT TO DO
THERE IS NO CURE
SORROW CUTS DEEP
RAINBOWS DON'T SHOW
BEAUTY HAS FADED
I HAVE TO GO
I'M FEELING RAGGED & SMALL
I HEARD A TEARDROP FALL
GOODBYE BABY GOODBYE

After four long, grueling, yet rewarding, days we had recorded two songs complete for *'The Essentials'* LP, *'Goodbye Baby'* and *'Sweet America 2018'*.

I had been living in a Holiday Inn Express, eating Indian and Malaysia food. I had ridden the bus to Turnpike Studios, both ways, each way took me forty five minutes. I was feeling tired and spent. I needed a treat. So, once through security, at Terminal five in London's Heathrow terminal, I decided to splurge on the Plaza Premium Lounge. In this posh place I would rub shoulders with the Business traveler and aristocrats. I would live *The Life of Riley* for two hours before my flight home to Lori. I felt I had earned a little comfort.

The lounge website reads, *'it allows the elite traveller to relax and refresh before departure'*. It provided, *'unlimited high-speed Wi-Fi, shower facilities, and delicious food and beverages'*, but the coup de grâce was the pleasant surprise awaiting me inside the airport. I was at the coffee dispenser with my bone china cup in hand, when I realized that the guy standing next to me, with a plate of nigiri sushi, was Taylor Hawkins. Taylor was the drummer of the rock band Foo Fighters.

I said,

'hello',

Taylor smiled and asked me if I was going to try the sushi. I said that I would, after I woke up a bit, which explained the black coffee. I told Taylor that I recognised him, and that I too was a musician and songwriter. I then politely asked if he would like to join me at my table. He agreed.

The conversation began with me telling Taylor that my daughter, and I, attended the Vancouver 1996 Allanis Morissette concert date, he was Morissette's drummer that night. It was my daughter's second live concert, she was thirteen. The first concert we shared was New Kids on the Block, a few years earlier. I bought her the t-shirt. I told Taylor that his drumming, and the entire band, plus the genius, that is Allanis, was a strong memory for both of us. A great night that my kid and I, still talk about, from time to time. Again, I bought her the t-shirt.

Taylor shared with me a telephone call that he received from Allanis in '96 inviting him to join the band; the rehearsals; how great she was; and how he loved the tour. The band's mandate and blueprint from Allanis was, *'We are not duplicating the sound, or the arrangements, of 'Jagged Little Pill', we are reinventing it'.* Morissette and the album won six Juno Awards, and five Grammies.

Macartney and I have shared some brilliant concerts over the decades. Joe Bonamassa, Paul McCartney, Art Garfunkel and No Doubt. We never saw a bad one, but Allanis was a watershed night for her. The volume, the intensity and the crowd. The audience was heavily female, and they were there to party. Macartney's father knew how to behave, which meant let her be, and I watched my kid drink it in.

Taylor Hawkins stood out that night, much like I witnessed when Joe English was superb on the kit with McCartney in 1976, and Keith Moon captured the night when I saw The Who in 1968. Taylor Hawkins was one of the world's best rock drummers. We were sitting, chatting, sipping coffee, when our duo became a trio in the Plaza Premium Lounge at London Heathrow Airport, Terminal 5.

'Hi, I'm David, can I join you guys, sounds like we're talking music?'

It was David Grohl. The Fighters leader, and the ex-drummer of Nirvana. David explained that the Fighters had flown to England, the previous day, to film a BBC Live concert in the west-midlands. It did not go as well as planned. They laughed about the never-ending technical issues that they faced in Birmingham rain.

I think talking to a fresh face, mine, was a positive for these two road-rats. Their lives being an unending road trip around the world. Fun, but a lot of hurry-up-and-wait. We all were in that lounge, waiting.

David explained to me how Taylor had joined the Foo Fighters in 1997.

Grohl called Hawkins, an acquaintance at the time, seeking his recommendations for a new drummer to join the band. Grohl was under the impression that Hawkins would not want to leave Morissette's touring

band, given she was a bigger act than Foo Fighters at the time. To Grohl's surprise, however, Hawkins volunteered to join the band himself,

explaining that he wanted to be a drummer in a rock band rather than for a solo act. A great story. To me truth always tops fiction.

Taylor became the # 2 in the Foo Fighters hierarchy for the next 25 years. He shared media duties, vocals, and some writing with David. The band grew into an arena act loved by the younger, and heavier, music aficionado. They were respected and loved by this demographic. Over the decades Grohl worked with McCartney, Slash, Brian May, and many others on side-projects. He is a giant in today's industry. We talked a lot about the ever-changing music business. They were interested in my 1973 *Blue Sky* LP, and found the players I employed, Larry Carlton, Jim Gordon, Larry Knechtel and Joe Osborn, who were twenty-five years senior to them, interesting. They questioned me at length. I enjoyed being the elder statesman.

Taylor told me that Jim Gordon, my LA drummer most famously known as the guy from Derek and the Dominoes, who co-wrote Layla, being a personal hero. Jim hit the kit hard like Taylor does in the Fighters, and as David always did when he was Nirvana's drummer. Drummers are unique, like hockey goalies and surgeons. A little different.

David shared how much he loved playing live, loved recording and writing, and how much he loved the road. Taylor was a home body, when he could be, and he had recorded three solo LPs. Time flew by, and ne'er a moment was silent.

My British Airways flight, BA 85, London to Vancouver, was announced. The ten hours in limbo awaited me.

Taylor and I quickly exchanged e mails, and we stayed in touch after that encounter. He sent me a Hawkins LP, and I shared a digital copy of *Blue Sky*. Nice reviews went both ways.

It was enjoyable. A lovely way to fill time with two lovely gentlemen. We loved the ninety minutes. I am so happy I went to Lounge at London Heathrow Airport, Terminal 5.

Footnote:

Why did Dave Grohl choose the name Foo Fighters for his band? Grohl had a fascination with unidentified flying objects and UFO books at the time, and the term 'Foo Fighter' was used by Allied aircraft pilots during World War II to describe UFOs or mysterious aerial phenomena.

We lost Taylor in 2022, at the young age of fifty. He died in a Four Seasons Hotel room, in Bogota Columbia. The toxicology report was a hard read.

Tidbit six

Lennon Phone Call

Sunset lit the sky. It was 6.05pm on a Sunday night, it was 27 May 1969, and I was in my Kitsilano bedroom. I was 18. That night an excited me spent three minutes on the telephone with John Lennon. This unreal moment in time, and this eventful conversation, came about because Lennon was with Ono in their Montréal bed-in, accepting telephone calls from across Canada.

Lennon and Ono had secured rooms 1738, 1740, 1742 and 1744 in Montréal's Queen Elizabeth Hotel for seven nights, and this night number two of their Montréal bed-in. Vancouver radio announced in the early afternoon, that listeners could call the station and speak to John Lennon in Montréal at 6pm Pacific time. It was out-of-the-blue, so extraordinary, and a little unbelievable, but it was real. At six sharp I called the telephone number offered. A voice asked my name:

'Barry Greenfield'.
'Barry, you are number one.'

To my surprise and glee, I heard that I would be connected in five minutes. I was the first to get accepted, and apparently, I would be the first to speak to the Beatle. An angel sat on my shoulder. I am so often blown away by simply trying things, expecting nothing, and then arriving at a positive outcome. Ask and you shall receive. I had nothing prepared. I had given little thought to what I could, or would say, I simply waited, numb, nervous, and continuously looking at my watch, every few seconds. A year earlier I had sat in Apple Headquarter, in London, auditioning. That was a lifetime ago, and I was about to talk to Lennon on the telephone.

I lived in a shared communal hippie house on west second avenue in Vancouver. The bedroom was a large top floor typical bachelor pad, with musical touches on the walls. My guitar sat on the bed, always ready.

I was on hold for John Lennon. I was still not convinced that it was real, or happening.

The couples first bed-in was held in Amsterdam. John and Yoko's second bed-in was planned to take place in New York, but John could not enter the US because of his cannabis-bust a year earlier. First, they flew to the Bahamas but after spending one night in the heat, they decided to fly to my homeland, Canada. They wanted to be near New York for better press coverage, so they chose Montréal, a City with close proximity to New York. They *set up shop* at The Queen Elizabeth Hotel at 900 René-Lévesque Blvd Ouest, Montreal in Room 1742, That would be their headquarters from May 26 to June 2, 1969.

'Connecting you now!'

'Hello, what's your name?' was what I heard.

It sounded like John. It was John. The telephone line was clear, no static, and that was unusual on long-distance calls in 1969. I imagine it was relayed through the radio stations in Vancouver and Montréal.

'Barry'.

'Where are You calling from?' he asked.

'Vancouver'.

I told John that I was always impressed with the way he used his songwriting, and his esteemed position to spread his political views. I mentioned my admiration for his song, *'Revolution'*. I continued by adding that I was a simple teenager attending Simon Fraser University, and therefore I had no impact on things globally. He was an important player in the world. I added that I had followed his bed-in in Amsterdam, something that a person of his stature could do and gain worldwide attention through it. It was interesting to me. Unique. Me, it was so different. How can anyone unknown like me make a difference? John listened to me and replied in a clear succinct voice. A man who was used to communicating clearly and getting to the point. He simply said,

'Barry, we are all one. Everything everyone does has impact. Your actions, everyday are as important to this planet, as are mine. Your work is needed. We all must try to change things. We are all able to help, Barry'.

It was so simple. I was truly moved by his basic response. John then spoke in some detail about reduce, recycle, reuse. How if I did that everyday the impact on the world would be truly significant. It was super interesting how John spoke to me as an equal. He was respectful and kind. This was a Beatle sitting in a hotel bed in Montréal and I never felt rushed by him. It was not a lecture. It was a conversation. He gave me a few minutes, and he listened patiently to me, and when he spoke, I felt connected.

This is not a significant story. This is not a groundbreaking epiphany moment. It was but a lovely moment in time for me. I remember it with great fondness. I share it here because it moved the rudder a degree, and my boat sailed to a different location.

All because John Lennon took the time to talk to a fan and share a thought with a student of his music, in 1969.

I am now seventy-four. I still have all my marbles. I still laugh, cry, think, and grow. I look into the rear-view mirror, and I see a satisfied life. I see things that I accomplished that were of value. I see that I made errors too many times, but no one got hurt.

My family is strong, loving, intelligent and succeeding. Music is still arriving. New songs I perform from the heart. I perform live shows twice a year, and the response is wonderful. I love the blend I chose, Financial Planner, songwriter and family man. Recently I have placed music in three film projects. BBC, Australia Film, and HBO. That's an avenue I will explore more. I am an author.

The chat with John Lennon in 1969 was another brick in the wall. Every brick makes the wall stronger; every brick makes the wall more beautiful, and every brick makes the wall more interesting.

I crossed paths twice in my life with Lennon. 1968 at Apple, when I offered a recording contract by John, and now in 1969. Both connections changed me.

I listen to The Beatles two hundred days a year. I still learn from the band, I still enjoy their writing and records, I still am amazed.

Footnote: *As is shared frequently by me. If you see a chance take it.*

On December 8th, 1980, John was murdered at the Dakota in New York. Shot five times. Brutal. I was driving home from a meeting, and was on the Lions Gate bridge in Vancouver, when the radio announcer shard the news, it was 10.30pm. I never slept that night. I received, and I made dozens of telephone calls to friends, to talk. The next day I turned thirty, December 9th, 1980. I never celebrated that milestone. I was in shock for a few day. We all were. We had lost a guide. A writer of great worth. A man who understood and shared so much. John Lennon.

The B side on my 1972 hit 'New York is Closed Tonight', was a song I wrote in 1969 for John, 'John Roll On'.

>A brothers a brother
>But Yoko's a lover
>And brother you love her a lot
>John roll on

John left us much.

>As soon as you're born they make you feel small
>By giving you no time instead of it all
>'Til the pain is so big you feel nothing at all
>A working class hero is something to be
>A working class hero is something to be
>Keep you doped with religion and sex and TV
>And you think you're so clever and classless and free
>But you're still fucking peasants as far as I can see
>A working class hero is something to be
>A working class hero is something to be
>If you want to be a hero, well, just follow me

Epilogue

Blue Sky was the perfect storm.

- ✓ *Solid songwriting.* Recorded in the summer of 1973 when I was 22. The world of Pop music was maturing, heading into a second decade, following in the footsteps that the sixties delivered. The songs that dominated radio shaped our thinking about the single. But with *'Rubber Soul'* in 1965, the importance of the LP arrived and we never looked back. Kids like me were students, studying at the feet of the elders: Townsend, Davies, Lennon, Cohen, Dylan, Mitchell, Waters, Richards, and McCartney.

- ✓ *A AAA-plus arranger.* *Blue Sky* had Jimmie Haskell, the arranger who understood how to create silk out of cotton. I took my twelve songs and I moved into the Haskell home. We worked ten hours a day, for three days, sharpening, tightening, and improving.

- ✓ *An appreciative and motivated Producer.* David M. Kershenbaum. His first project. I chose David over others with better pedigrees. I followed my heart. David went on to win Grammies, Oscars and more. *Blue Sky* is a duet between me and David.

- ✓ *A world class studio with engineers to match.* The two engineers were Elvis's engineers. The room, Studio B, was the one the King used in LA. I stood where he stood. They showed me the exact spot because I asked them to. They showed great patience with me, a novice and beginner.

- ✓ *Musicians.* *Blue Sky* had the best players on the planet: Carlton, Gordon, Osborn, Muhoberac, Knechtel, Kunkel and Estes.

- *Enthusiasm, no fear, love and heart.* I was unspoiled by life. I was having fun. I was eager, and willing, to experiment. Plus, the songs on *Blue Sky* were good; an essential component. The track sequencing was excellent; an important attribute. The entire experience was a joy to everyone. It shows in the tracks to this very day. First albums are frequently the finest in the canon. Why? Because the artist is not emulating past success. The artist is creating something original.

I quit the business before I should. But I have zero regrets. It all played out magnificently on *Blue Sky*.

Acknowledgements

'My Journey to Blue Sky' was written for the side table on my wife's side of the bed, for the bookshelf in my granddaughter's bedroom, for my daughter's home, and the friends all over our planet that I love.

Thanks go from my heart to the following who have all made their own invaluable contributions to enable me to document the story of my journey to Blue Sky.

My wife, Lori, who has encouraged me throughout this endeavour, picked me up when things were not going so well health wise, and has put up with me both night and day over the last 24 months or so of writing this account.

My Mom and Dad who were always there for me in my youth. Thank you from the bottom of my heart.

My sister Suzan Greenfield who has been a rock to lean on for all our lives and who has never wavered in her belief in me and my work.

Macartney and Graham, my kids who are the Everest of my planet.

Navy, my granddaughter who brings her Grandma Yote and Zaida the ultimate joy. A teacher already, age three and a bit.

Red and Andrea, who end every conversation with, 'I Love You'.

My old school friend, and fellow Mancunian, Mike Topper who has read this work, helped me with the layout and grammar, suggested areas of improvement and generally functioned as a sounding board throughout this project. A piece of the puzzle that came from out of nowhere to make everything in this read better.

All my friends and fellow musicians all over the world who have been there to lend their valuable experience of both the music and business world in support of this work. To my fellow musicians and friends, Dave Kell, Chris Nole, Charles Donavon, Adrian Woodward, Shane Fontayne, Steve Holbrook, Joe Isaacs, Jack Pearson, Dow Tomlin, Chris Brown, Graham Gouldman, John Lennon, Larry Carlton, Russ Kunkel, Jim Gordon, Larry Muhoberac, Gene Estes, Joe Osborn, Rick Ruggieri, Peter Abbot, Peter Tattersall, Hymie and Betty Gouldman, Eric Stewart, Lol Crème, Kevin Godley, Claire Lawrence, Teddie Dahlin, Fiona McQuarrie, Chris Webb, Mike Finkel, Derek Taylor, Harvey Lisberg, Philip Lisberg, Bob Buckley, Jeff Gort, Gary Robinson, Dr. Janice Crook, Cam McCubbin, Mike Bodayle, Bill Buckingham, Neil Loomer, Gaye Delorme, John Lee Hooker, 10cc, Simon Crum, Dick Jane, Mike Kirby, David Sinclair, David Goldman, Alex Chan. Jeff Ridley, Cindy Wine, Bill McAvoy, Mick Dalla-Vee, Clay Hagel, TJ, Roxy, Tia, Sisy, Denali, Printer and Navy Emmeline Dot Snowfield. Thank you all for all you have done and the encouragement that you have all shown. This book is so much better because of you all. Thank you.

Barry Greenfield
Vancouver BC
barrygreenfield@shaw.ca

www.ingramcontent.com/pod-product-compliance
Ingram Content Group UK Ltd.
Pitfield, Milton Keynes, MK11 3LW, UK
UKHW031020120325
4954UKWH00009B/307